ParaReading
A Training Guide for Tutors

Participant's Workbook

Deborah R. Glaser, Ed.D.

Sopris West™
EDUCATIONAL SERVICES

A Cambium Learning Company

A LETRS Supplement Module

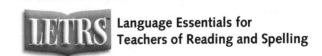

Language Essentials for
Teachers of Reading and Spelling

ISBN 1-59318-729-7

Printed in the United States of America

Published and Distributed by

Sopris West™
EDUCATIONAL SERVICES

A Cambium Learning Company

4093 Specialty Place • Longmont, Colorado 80504 • (303) 651-2829
www.sopriswest.com

146546/258/8-06

Acknowledgments

For several of my teaching years, I was fortunate to have paraeducators at my side, working with me and assisting me with my teaching and the multiple daily tasks teachers face. I learned numerous lessons from these generous and caring individuals. One of those lessons was that if I taught *them* well, these successful paraeducators ended up leaving me and returning to college to get their teaching certificates! It was always difficult to say goodbye, but these were joyous occasions too, because these individuals had experienced the positive results of appropriately designed reading instruction with their students. They were proof that knowledgeable, well-trained tutors can make a difference in young children's reading skills.

Paraeducators deserve training that incorporates current scientifically based research to help them be the strongest reading tutors they can be. Students deserve to learn from tutors who understand the reading process and what and how to teach, so that not a moment is lost in becoming a reader. I wish the many paraeducators who complete this training countless joyful successes in the work they do with young children and in their collaborative efforts with classroom teachers.

Louisa Moats and Steve Mitchell of Sopris West are stars in my life. I thank them for recognizing the critical need for qualified paraeducators and for giving me the opportunity to produce this training guide. Thank you for being my teacher, Louisa; I never fail to learn something new from you. And thank you Holly Bell at Sopris West for being the cheerleader who encouraged and supported my efforts throughout!

About the Author

Deborah Glaser, Ed.D., is an educational consultant and trainer based in Boise, Idaho. She brings 28 years of teaching experience to her current work with schools, teachers, and reading program development. Deborah wrote the *Comprehensive Literacy Plan* on which Idaho's Reading Initiative was based, and she has trained thousands of teachers across the country on the foundations of learning to read and how to teach reading effectively so that *all* children learn. She is a national trainer for *Language Essentials for Teachers of Reading and Spelling* (LETRS) and *Dynamic Indicators of Basic Early Literacy Skills* (DIBELS). *ParaReading* was developed to assist with filling the need for qualified tutors who understand the underlying reading skills young children need and how to teach them. Her professional interests include building professional learning communities through collaboration, with a focus on improving reading skills for all children, and evaluating professional development in ways that reflect teacher learning and student achievement.

Contents

Introduction

A Need for Trained Reading Tutors

The demand for well-informed, trained, and knowledgeable educators and paraeducators[1] is greater than it has ever been. Paraeducators play a critical and significant role in schools and learning centers as a support to the teaching and learning process. Current statistics from the U.S. Department of Education reveal that, in 87% of Title 1 schools, paraeducators are assigned the responsibility of teaching reading (U.S. Department of Education, 1999). This dependence on paraeducators demands the attention of teachers, school administrators, and parents. Have we prepared our paraeducators to implement proven teaching practices that will promote successful levels of student achievement and reading ability? Schools are increasingly responsive to calls for scientific, research-based reading instruction. It is important that all reading instructors, including paraeducators, know how young children learn to read and that they are trained in how to implement best practices to ensure that *all* children become readers.

Legislation under the No Child Left Behind Act (2001) addresses the paraeducators' role and requires that they receive training to support the application of scientifically researched principles of reading instruction. Research with trained paraeducators demonstrates that the educational community can have high expectations for the paraeducator as reading tutor. Trained paraeducators using a structured program can be as effective as experts with advanced degrees (Elbaum, Vaughn, Hughes, & Moody, 2000; Vadasy, Jenkins, & Pool, 2000). These findings intensify the need for paraeducator training that addresses the core reading components and provides the essential knowledge of both *what* to teach and *how* to teach reading to young children.

ParaReading provides thoughtful and well-designed materials for formal paraeducator training. This training ensures that tutors are indeed qualified to implement structured reading programs and to assist teachers with the instruction of students who are at risk in reading and spelling. *ParaReading* offers the crucial training to enrich, strengthen, and build a resource for sustainable and strategic instruction, so that all children learn to read.

---

[1] The term "paraeducator" was purposefully chosen for this publication because it describes most clearly the role of paraprofessional, volunteer, tutor, and classroom assistant. *Paraeducator* references a level of expertise in the education field in the same way that *paralegal* does in the field of law.

Basis for ParaReading Content

ParaReading bases its curriculum on the National Reading Panel's key instructional recommendations (Report of the National Reading Panel, 2000). These key reading skill components—phonemic awareness, decoding (or phonics), fluency, vocabulary, and comprehension—are presented within an instructional design that establishes a strong base for knowledge, application, and implementation of these five comprehensive reading program elements. Supplementary training is also included in maintaining records of students' performance, handling student errors effectively, and communicating with supervisors. A knowledgeable paraeducator has the potential to strengthen any elementary classroom's reading program.

The ParaReading Workbook and the Training Manual and Presentation Kit

ParaReading materials are available in two parts:

1. *ParaReading*: A Training Guide for Tutors, Participant's Workbook

2. *ParaReading*: A Training Guide for Tutors, Trainer's Workbook and Presentation Kit.

It is necessary for every paraprofessional attending training to have a copy of the participant workbook. The *ParaReading* Training Manual and Presentation Kit contains the training materials necessary to train paraeducators: a complete text with the participant materials in the front section and a trainer's section in the back, which mirrors the workbook page numbers with pertinent training procedures and script. The Presentation Kit also contains a Power Point presentation, Transparency presentation, and handouts.

Research Base for ParaReading

Research utilizing twelve single-case studies highlights the instructional effectiveness of paraeducators trained in the foundation of how young children learn to read and how to apply specific instructional methods (Glaser, 2002). High school senior tutors completed explicit background training and applied a systematic four-step lesson teaching three of the five research-based components: phonemic awareness, decoding, and fluency.

Each tutor worked with two different students for six weeks. Oral reading fluency measures were gathered (Edformation, 2002) every two weeks for twelve weeks throughout this experiment. Baseline, treatment, and post-treatment data were compared using a statistical method determined to be sensitive to individual changes across outcome measures when moderately few data points are available (Mueser, Yarnold, & Foy, 1991). Five students demonstrated significant gains in reading fluency, and additional analysis revealed that all students (N = 12) made increases, averaging 2.5 words per week, in words read per minute. These findings are comparable to a similar, seven-week study utilizing certified classroom and special education teachers (Hasbrouk, Ihnot, & Rogers, 1999), where students made between a 1.23 and 2.35 words-per-week gain.

These and other studies demonstrate that trained, noncertified tutors can improve reading fluency (Elbaum et al., 2000). Gains in reading fluency, measured by words read correct per minute, have been highly correlated with improved comprehension (Shinn, Deno, & Fuchs, 2002); fluency gains match up with overall reading gains. By placing *trained* paraeducators with students at risk of reading failure, schools increase opportunities for successful tutoring experiences where students improve reading skills and bolster their self-esteem and confidence in their abilities. Schools that utilize *trained* tutors to support classroom teachers' instruction increase the chances for students to learn in small groups where the learning and the instructional pace can be monitored for greater gains.

The educational community is increasing its use of paraeducators to tutor greater numbers of students who are at risk and low performing in reading (Cohen, Kulik, & Kulik, 1982). Paraeducators make a vital contribution to successful reading programs, but key to their success is intentional training in the process of how children learn to read and how to implement proven teaching practices. *ParaReading* provides core training intended to improve the efforts of reading tutors and the abilities of the children they teach.

Welcome to the Paraeducator

Welcome to *ParaReading*. This paraeducator training will prepare you to be a confident, knowledgeable reading tutor who is available to help children, their families, and the personnel with whom you work. Children benefit from the relationships you build with them because students who work one-on-one with caring tutors demonstrate improved self-esteem and confidence (Wasik, 1998; Fitzgerald, 2001). Families profit when their children, who are at risk of academic failure, begin to succeed and gain confidence as learners. And schools and learning centers need paraeducators to provide the needed manpower to reach all children. As a paraeducator, you are a very valuable person and perform a very important role. The goals (broad-based learning) and objectives (action-oriented, observable outcomes) for your *ParaReading* training are listed on the next page.

LETRS   Reflection

1. Discuss what guides reading instruction done by paraeducators in your school.

2. What goals do you have for this training?

3. What do you think would make your current practice more effective?

Goals

♦ Understand the important roles that phonemic awareness, phonics (or decoding), fluency, vocabulary, and comprehension have in reading instruction.

♦ Learn how to apply systematic and direct practices to teach students the five basic components of reading.

♦ Acquire specific instructional, record-keeping, and tutorial management skills.

Objectives

Effective paraeducators:

♦ Observe modeling of instructional techniques and instructional content and participate in role-playing during the training.

♦ Demonstrate mastery of the explicit systematic learning that strengthens effective reading instruction.

♦ Deliver praise, encouragement, positive feedback, and reinforcement as part of their successful instruction.

♦ Recognize areas in which students need extra help, and understand the importance of communicating observations to supervisors when there are questions or concerns.

♦ Utilize error-correction procedures that are quick, simple, and consistently applied.

♦ Keep accurate records as an assessment of a student's progress, of their work, and for program evaluation.

To further strengthen your training, suggestions for data collection, organization, how to respond to student errors, and communication with supervising teachers are included in the Tutor's Tips section of this workbook, along with additional instructional advice. In the Tutor's Tips section, you will also find Strategy Reference Cards, the tutor strategies that you learn in this training formatted for use as a quick teaching reference!

Format

The Paraeducator's Workbook presents each of the five reading components in its own chapter designed to help you become familiar with the component and how to teach it. Your lessons will follow this consistent format:

♦ **Discussion**—Each chapter begins with a discussion of the focus component. Your trainer will present background information and research, so that you will understand the importance of the skill being taught.

♦ **Your Turn to Learn**—Your Turn to Learn provides opportunities for you to practice and perfect your own reading skills in the area of focus. Paraeducators may have their skills assessed during this section.

♦ **How to Teach It**—Procedures for teaching the focus skill are presented in this section. Necessary instructional materials are listed, and a data collection process is described.

♦ **Practice It**—Before you teach any reading skill, you should have lots of practice! The training allows time to observe, practice in pairs, and role-play with other tutors and the trainer.

♦ **Review**—A brief review assessment completes each chapter. These reviews are meant to provide helpful feedback to you and your trainer as you progress through the training.

Note to the Paraeducator   When we teach, it is natural to assume that our students will learn using the same methods and tools that *our* teachers used when we were learning. It is important to put aside your memories of how you learned and even how your own children learned as you begin this training. Research provides the key to helping us design and deliver instruction that works for the majority of kids at risk (Foorman, Francis, Fletcher, Schatschneider, & Mehta 1998; Moats, 1999). *ParaReading* uses this research as the basis for training you to implement effective, proven reading practices. Good luck! You are on your way to becoming a *ParaReading* tutor and to giving the gift of reading to the children you teach!

ParaReading Training

Content

ParaReading training is based upon five critical components of reading instruction. These components can be illustrated as five points on a star:

Before We Begin

Exercise

Consider your previous encounters with a child who had difficulty learning to read. Who comes to mind? A boy or a girl? How old? What were some of this child's experiences with learning to read?

Use colored markers and a piece of paper to draw the person you're thinking of. It doesn't have to be a work of art ready to hang in a museum; the critical thing here is that you create an image of the person who will represent why you want to learn how to effectively help children improve their reading.

Write about your person:

1. Tell about why you chose this person.

2. Tell about an event you recall that illustrates the difficulty this person had with learning to read.

_____

_____

_____

_____

_____

_____

_____

_____

_____

_____

_____

_____

_____

Post your drawing in an area of the room set aside by your trainer. Look at all of the pictures of all of the children. Imagine that they are your students while you learn *ParaReading*!

Chapter 1: Phonemic Awareness

Discussion

> **Exercise #1:** Listen and respond as your trainer asks you to answer some simple word-play tasks.

The tasks that you just completed require a linguistic skill called *phonemic awareness*. Phonemic awareness happens in the absence of visual letters. The listener's focus is on oral language, on speech sounds.

The ability to separate and produce speech sounds in words requires one to have phonemic awareness, or awareness of the speech sounds in one's own language. This ability seems simple to us, yet to many young children the questions you were asked are not easy to answer. Phonemic awareness is one of the critical skills that enable young children to decode written language into spoken language and read!

If you ask a young child who is preparing to enter first grade, "What are you going to learn in school?", the answer will invariably be, "I am going to learn to read!" First grade is where we gain entrance into the world of reading. School is where we learn to read. Reading is what opens worlds to us; reading is what older brothers and sisters, friends, and parents can do, and, now, "I am going to learn to read too!"

Unfortunately, though, reading does not come easily to about 40% of children (Vellutino & Scanlon, 1987). They watch anxiously as others in their class begin to make sense of those letters on a page, while it remains a struggle to them. Slowly, over time, if they do not "catch on," these struggling children become frustrated; confidence is lost, and they feel "dumb." In fact, most of these children simply lack a skill that can be taught to them: *phonemic awareness*!

A few years ago, children showed up on the first day of school and teachers would show them the letter "A" and instruct, "This letter says /a/ as in *apple*." Educators assumed something very critical to the process of reading. They assumed that children were able to conceptualize the individual sounds of their language and isolate individual sounds from the other sounds in a word. Educators have learned that many children—two out of five—are not able to do this when they enter first grade and many who continue to make slow progress in reading persist with low levels of speech-sound awareness. Without this ability to identify sounds and to separate and blend speech sounds within their language, children have serious difficulty with decoding and, consequently, learning to read.

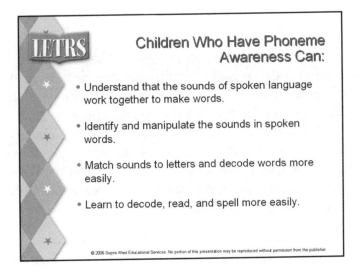

Phonemes are the basic building blocks of spoken language. They are the separate speech sounds that, when combined in seamless streams, create the language we so effortlessly use to communicate. The awareness that speech is composed of sounds that can be isolated from each other has proven to be one of the most fundamental skills for young readers to possess.

Tutors Know! *Phoneme*: a speech sound. Phonemic awareness allows one to identify the speech sounds in words. Examples: "There are three speech sounds in house—/h/ /ow/ /s/." "The last sound in book is /k/."

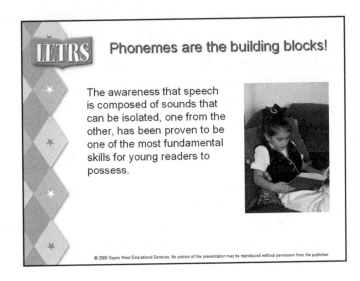

Your Turn to Learn

When you teach young children to read, it is important to be able to understand and sympathize with what they are experiencing. You are a reader. This makes it a challenge to understand students' experiences as they learn to read or work to improve their reading skills. It is critical to recognize that many of the students with whom you will work do not yet have a concept of the individual sounds, the *phonemes*, that make up the words that they read and speak. They have not yet developed phonemic awareness, and this may make learning to read difficult.

Your own phonemic awareness may not be as well developed as it needs to be to teach reading to young and struggling readers. Many adults need practice. This section will prepare you to include phoneme instruction in your lessons by building your *personal* understanding of phonemic awareness.

> **Tutors Know!** When you see a letter inside of two marks, like /m/, you say the sound represented by the letter, not the letter name.

What Phonemic Awareness Is

Phonemes are the individual sounds that combine to create the language we speak. For example, the sounds /t/, /ă/, and /k/ are separate sounds that we create with our tongues, teeth, and throats, and they can be arranged in a certain order to create the word *cat*. There are 43 different phonemes in the English language. Every language has a unique set of phonemes.

The following chart presents the 43 phonemes and examples of the sounds in words. The phonemes are divided into consonant sounds and vowel sounds. Practice saying these sounds with your trainer. When you say the sounds, be very careful not to add an additional separate sound, /ŭ/, to these sounds. Say /b/, not /buh/. Notice these characteristics when you practice saying the sounds:

♦ Feel your throat as you say each consonant sound. Do you feel a vibration? Is the sound a "voiced" sound or an "unvoiced" sound? Be careful! You will discover that there are sounds you may be voicing when in fact they are voiceless!

♦ Use a mirror. What is your tongue doing when you say the sounds? Is it tapping somewhere in your mouth? Is it flattened? In the back of your mouth or in the front?

♦ Which sounds share similar articulation features?

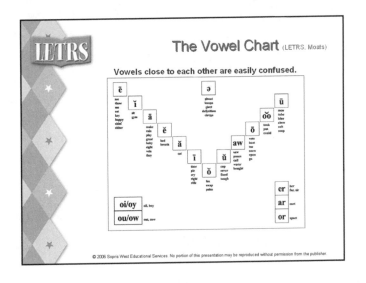

Consonant Sounds			Vowel Sounds		
1.	/b/	butter	26.	/e/	see
2.	/p/	pet	27.	/ĭ/	sit
3.	/m/	mouse	28.	/a/	make
4.	/f/	fuzz	29.	/ĕ/	bed
5.	/v/	vest	30.	/ă/	cat
6.	/th/	think	31.	/i/	time
7.	/<u>th</u>/	them	32.	/ŏ/	fox
8.	/t/	tiger	33.	/ŭ/	cup
9.	/d/	desk	34.	/aw/	saw, call, water, bought
10.	/n/	nose	35.	/o/	vote
11.	/s/	smile	36.	/oo/	book
12.	/z/	zipper	37.	/u/	tube, moo
13.	/sh/	ship	38.	/ə/ (schwa)	about, lesson
14.	/zh/	measure	39.	/oi/	oil, boy
15.	/ch/	chair	40.	/ou/	out, cow
16.	/j/	judge	41.	/er/	her, fur, sir
17.	/k/	kite	42.	/ar/	car
18.	/g/	goat	43.	/or/	corn
19.	/ng/	sang			
20.	/y/	yellow			
21.	/wh/	whistle			
22.	/w/	wagon			
23.	/h/	hand			
24.	/l/	lion			
25.	/r/	rose			

Exercise #2: Practice saying these sounds with a partner and for your trainer.

Turn to the LETRS consonant and vowel articulation charts in the back of your workbook. Now, practice saying the sounds again using these charts as a reference.

Box the sounds that are sound pairs.

Tricky sounds abound when we start isolating them from the whole words we speak. These are a few that you will need to know because you are sure to run into them with your students. What is the surprise in each of these?

Quilt = /k/ /w/ /i/ /l/ /t/

Box = /b/ /ŏ/ /k/ /s/

Universe = /y/ /oo/ /n/ /ə/ /v/ /r/ /s/

Phonemic awareness is the awareness that our speech is made up of separate sounds. Phonemic awareness enables children to isolate the first sound, last sound, and middle sounds when they hear or say a word. It allows them to separate out all the phonemes in words and to match them to written symbols. *To think phonemically, is to consider the spoken sound separately from the letter we use to represent the sound in our written language.* This is difficult for adults who are readers! We automatically visualize letters in our minds when we hear speech sounds. Young readers must learn to match phoneme sequences to letter patterns. For many, the process of reading falls apart at the basic level of phonemic awareness.

Exercise #3: Review and Discuss

Turn to your partner, and ask and answer these questions: What is a phoneme? What is phonemic awareness? Why is phonemic awareness important for young children to have?

Work together to write your answers here.

_____

_____

_____

_____

_____

_____

Exercise #4: Test and Practice Your Phonemic Awareness

Do the following Phonemic Awareness Activities with your trainer.

Phoneme Matching

Read the first word in each line and isolate the sound that is represented by the underlined letter or letter cluster. Then select the word or words in the line that contain the same sound. Circle the words you select.

1.	h**oo**k	food	cloud	foot	sugar
2.	l**au**gh	faun	train	sauce	grand
3.	mi**ss**	does	nose	box	close
4.	ca**ge**	gym	game	gnat	hang
5.	thi**n**k	blunt	sling	drink	hang

Count the Phonemes

Count the number of phonemes in the following words:

through _____   loose _____   fox _____   knight _____

high _____   pitcher _____   judge _____   fir _____

pay _____   torch _____   strong _____   oil _____

wheat _____   quiet _____   vision _____   cream _____

Identification of Phonemes

Identify the third phoneme in the following words:

shoes _____   square _____   notched _____

night _____   vision _____   ox _____

sing _____   odor _____   walk _____

(continued) **Exercise #4:** Test and Practice Your Phonemic Awareness

Now, pair up with someone and do the following phoneme tasks with your partner.

Isolating Phonemes—Think of three additional words that have the same sound as the underlined letter or letters in each word. List them. Be ready to share your collections of words!

<u>i</u>tch	
th<u>ou</u>ght	
tr<u>ee</u>	
b<u>oy</u>	
b<u>ir</u>d	

Segmenting Phonemes—Segment and count the phonemes for each of the following words. Place a penny or other marker in each of the squares to represent each sound in the word. Record the number of sounds.

house ___							
friend ___							
shelf ___							
thought ___							
key ___							
youth ___							
fox ___							
knock ___							
scrunched ___							

(continued) **Exercise #4:** Test and Practice Your Phonemic Awareness

Note: The previous activity is commonly used to teach segmentation to young children. When teaching young children to segment, it is important to use one box for each sound in the words they segment.

Auditory Blending—Take turns with your partner and say the given word separated out into all of its individual sounds. Leave about one second between each sound and then ask your partner to identify the word. Do not look at the word if you are the partner who is listening!

Partner One: Separate the Sounds		Partner Two: Separate the Sounds	
Growth	/g/ /r/ /oe/ /th/	Swish	/s/ /w/ /i/ /sh/
Axe	/a/ /k/ /s/	Touch	/t/ /u/ /ch/
Swoop	/s/ /w/ /oo/ /p/	Phone	/f/ /oe/ /n/
Pitch	/p/ /i/ /ch/	Quick	/k/ /w/ /i/ /k/
Think	/th/ /i/ /ng/ /k/	Drum	/d/ /r/ /u/ /m/
Brook	/b/ /r/ /oo/ /k/	Chalk	/ch/ /o/ /k/

How to Teach It: Phonemic Awareness

By including purposeful attention to phonemes when you tutor struggling readers, you are building a base that they will use to improve decoding and spelling. Prepare to include phonemic awareness in your lessons by using the advice in this section!

You will not do *all* of the following activities with your students in one lesson, but do spend about four minutes of your instructional time specifically on teaching phonemic awareness.

Choose Your Words Carefully

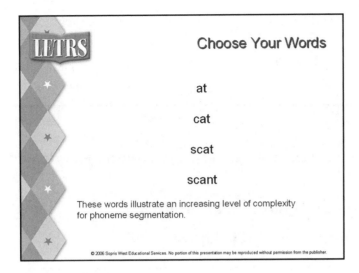

When you prepare to teach phonemic awareness, it is critical to consider and carefully choose the words you use. If your reading program provides lists of words for phoneme exercises, then you're set to go! If not, you will need to know how to match the words you choose with your students' phoneme ability level. Here are suggestions and examples of word choices that demonstrate an order of difficulty from simple to more complex.

1. Choose single-syllable words. The words provided by your school's reading program for reading practice are often the best to use for phonemic awareness activities too! Examples: *fan*, *pick*, *be*.

2. Use words beginning with continuant sounds for beginners. Examples /m/ and /s/.

3. If your student is beginning to isolate first and ending sounds, begin with words that have two or three sounds. For isolating middle sounds, make sure that your word choices are three-sound words. Examples: *cut*, *dirt*, *bead*.

4. Consonant digraphs (/th/, /sh/, etc.) represent one phoneme and are easily separated within words by early readers. Examples: *with*, *shot*, *chip*.

5. Avoid beginning- and ending-consonant blends until students can segment and blend words without blends. Then start with simple beginning two-sound blends. Examples: *blow*, *crutch*, *grace*. When students can segment beginning blends, use words with ending blends. Examples: *wind*, *milk*, *bent*.

6. Short and long vowel sounds are easier to segment than the vowel diphthongs (/ă/ is easier than /ow/). Examples: *dot, doze* as opposed to *shout, foil.*

Exercise #5

Place these words in order of simple to complex using the headings provided. Provide another example word for each item.

waist flap at graft chief shift

fact night moist pup broil froze swift

2 or 3 Sounds	Initial Blends	Ending Blends	Initial and Ending Blends	Vowel Diphthongs

---

Multisensory Instruction

Multisensory instruction means that students simultaneously see, hear, and touch what they are learning. Teach your students the following multisensory cues to get them involved and to make it fun!

Multisensory Cues

♦ *Tap the Sounds*—Beginning with your index finger, tap once for each sound as you move through each finger.

♦ *Tap Head, Waist, Ankles*—To help students isolate middle sounds, use three-sound words and tap your head for the first sound, your waist for the middle sound, and then reach down to your feet for the last sound.

♦ *Finger Count*—Count and say the sounds one at a time, raising a finger for each sound.

♦ *Pull the Sounds Out of Your Mouth*—Starting at your lips, pretend to grasp each isolated sound as you move your thumb and forefinger in a pulling movement away from your mouth.

♦ *Use Manipulatives*—Little crackers, paper squares, or game pieces make good visuals that can help young children see the segmentation as they separate the sounds in words.

Word Play—A Developmental Continuum

When teaching phonemic awareness, engage the child in *word play*. Phonemic awareness is developed along a continuum. Children initially learn to isolate first sounds in words, then ending sounds, and so on. Practice each of these with your trainer using your multisensory cues.

♦ *Isolate First Sounds*—Say the word and ask student to say the word and the first sound in that word. Repeat the word and sound with the student.

Example: You say, "House." Student says, "House, /h/." Together, you say, "House, /h/."

♦ *Isolate Last Sounds*—Say the word and ask the student to say the word and the last sound in that word. Repeat the word and the sound with the student.

Example: You say, "Jump." Student says, "Jump, /p/." Together, you say, "Jump, /p/."

♦ *Isolate Middle Sounds*—Say the word and ask the student to say the word and the middle sound in that word. Repeat the word and sound with the student. Three-sound words work best.

Example: You say, "Wave." Student says, "Wave, /ae/." Together, you say, "Wave, /ae/."

♦ *Segment All Sounds in a Word*—Say a word and ask the student to tell you all of the little sounds in that word.

Example: You say, "House." Student says, "House, /h/, /ou/, /s/." Together, you say, "House, /h/, /ou/, /s/."

◆ *Auditory Blending ("Secret Language")*—Say a word segmented into its isolated sounds, and ask the student to say the "secret word" back to you.

Example: You say, "/l/ /ee/ /f/." Student says, "Leaf."

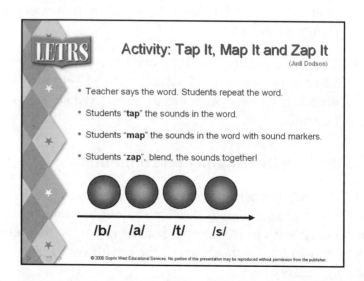

Tutors Know! *Complete Segmentation:* Separating all of the little sounds in a word—bead = /b//ee//d/. *Auditory Blending:* Blending the sounds of segmented word back into the whole word—/w//r//k/ = work!

Error Response

It is important to respond to students' errors in ways that will validate their efforts and draw attention to their errors as you correct them. Immediate feedback and correction will provide opportunities to increase learning.

1. Point out one thing that was done correctly. "Yes, the last sound is /t/."

2. Demonstrate the correct way. "Watch while I say all of the little sounds in the word: /m/ /ă/ /t/."

3. Point out the place where a correction was made. "There are two different sounds here, /m/ and /ă/, not one."

4. Student does it again with you. "Do it with me." If you're using sound markers, you and the student can pull down the sound markers together for each sound, saying the sounds as the markers are moved into the squares.

Data Recording

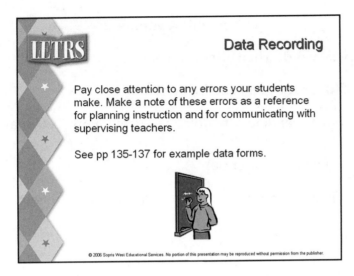

When you are teaching phonemic awareness, pay close attention to your students' responses. When errors are made, note what kinds of errors they are making:

♦ Are they able to do complete phoneme segmentation?

♦ Are they able to auditorially blend the phoneme-separated words that you give them?

♦ Are they confusing sounds? Example: saying /b/ for /p/, or /t/ for /d/.

♦ Do they consistently miss the last sounds or middle sounds in words?

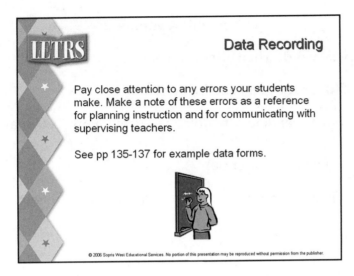

LETRS

Data Recording

Learn how to record student performance.

• Anecdotal notes – tell about tutoring sessions.

• Checklist – use an observation skill list.

• Specific feedback – supervisor may request specific feedback.

• Correct and error counts – record correct and error responses.

© 2006 Sopris West Educational Services. No portion of this presentation may be reproduced without permission from the publisher.

Use the following box as a sample recording form.

Phonemic Awareness

Provide words when discussing errors.

1. Student does this well: (circle)

   initial   ending   middle   segmentation   blending

2. Student errors: (circle)

   initial   ending   middle   segmentation   blending

3. Sound confusion?

A specific notation about a student's performance will be very valuable feedback to the student's teacher. You will be an important asset to the reading program when you provide feedback that will help determine instruction for students.

Practice It: Phonemic Awareness

Exercise #6:

Use the following story from the *Read Well* reading program (Sprick, Howard, & Fidanque, 1999). Find 10 one-syllable words to practice phonemic awareness instruction. Then form pairs and role-play student and tutor with each other. Practice phonemic-awareness instruction using word play and each of the multisensory cues. When you are in the student role, make a few intentional errors to give your partner practice with error handling and data recording.

Choose 10 single-syllable words from the story and write them here. Order your words from simple to complex. For example, words with two sounds will come before words with three sounds, and these will be followed by words with initial blends and words having final blends.

10 Words	Order the Words Simple to Complex
1. _____	_____
2. _____	_____
3. _____	_____
4. _____	_____
5. _____	_____
6. _____	_____
7. _____	_____
8. _____	_____
9. _____	_____
10. _____	_____

Funny Weather Facts

One summer day, in a small English town, clouds began to darken the sky. People expected an afternoon shower. However, when the rain started to fall it was more than just a shower. The people could hear funny sounds. Whack! Plop, plop, plop! Plop, plop, whack! Everyone ran indoors. Then they started to see funny things in the rain.

"What is happening?" the people asked.

A little kid said, "I think it's raining cats and dogs." Everyone laughed. A man said, "Maybe the sky is falling!" Another man asked, "Do you think it could be something from another planet?" Just then, someone else shouted, "Wow! That rain is hopping, and it's green!"

The people shouted all together, "It's raining frogs!"

Do you think this story is fact or fiction? It is an odd story, but it is a real story.

Reprinted by permission of the publisher from Marilyn Sprick, Lisa Howard, and Ann Fidanque, *Read Well Level One* (Longmont, CO: Sopris West, 2004), Unit 36, Story 3, 22, © 2004 by Sopris West.

(continued) **Exercise #6**

Use two of the words to practice teaching the following phonemic awareness tasks. List a multi-sensory cue you will use to teach each of the following skills. For example, you might select *Tap the Sounds* to isolate initial sounds.

♦ Isolate Initial Sounds _____

♦ Isolate Final Sounds _____

♦ Isolate Middle Vowel Sounds _____

♦ Complete Segmentation _____

♦ Auditory Blending _____

Error Response:

1. Point out one thing that was done correctly.

2. Demonstrate the correct way.

3. Point out the place where a correction was made. Explain.

4. Student does it again with you, together.

Data Record:

Phonemic Awareness

Provide words when discussing errors.

1. Student does this well: (circle)

   initial   ending   middle   segmentation   blending

2. Student errors: (circle)

   initial   ending   middle   segmentation   blending

3. Sound confusion?

Review: Phonemic Awareness

1. On what reading skill is Chapter 1 based? _____

2. Why is this a critical skill? _____

   _____

   _____

   _____

   _____

   _____

   _____

3. Where will you find words to use for teaching phonemic awareness? How will you know which are the best words to choose and use for phoneme awareness lessons? _____

   _____

   _____

   _____

   _____

   _____

   _____

   _____

   _____

4. Describe two procedures for teaching phonemic awareness. _____

   _____

   _____

   _____

   _____

   _____

   _____

(continued) **Review:** Phonemic Awareness

5. What do you do if your student makes an error? _____

_____

_____

_____

_____

_____

_____

_____

_____

6. Be ready to demonstrate your ability to segment and blend phonemes with your trainer.

Chapter 2: Phonics

Discussion

A young or struggling reader faces tasks similar to those of a detective. Detectives decode mysteries, and readers decode words. Fortunately for readers, there is a consistent set of sounds that can be applied to letters and groups of letters to solve their mysteries. This application of sounds to letters to decode words is called *phonics*. We learned about *phonemic awareness* in the first chapter. Now we will take those same sounds and map them onto the letters, or *graphemes*, that are used to visually represent those sounds.

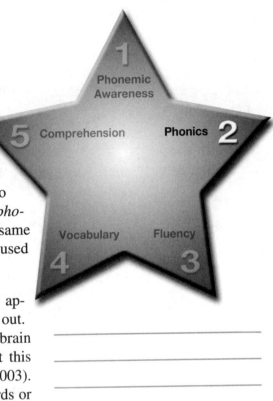

Studies have shown that the first strategy proficient readers apply when they come across an unfamiliar word is to sound it out. Studies that compare poor readers' brain activity with the brain activity of accomplished readers demonstrate how difficult this decoding process is for the struggling reader (Shaywitz, 2003). We also know that when students spend time analyzing words or decoding them, they are more likely to automatically recall that word the next time they come across it. Phonics, or decoding, is the application of analysis that originates from the basic structure of our written language.

Your school will most likely provide you with reading material that requires the teaching of phonics. The reading lessons may be direct and clearly outlined with a script to follow, or they may be vague, with little direction provided for phonics instruction. This wide possible range of instructional support requires that you be prepared and confident in your phonics skills and that you know how to apply basic instruction to help young readers improve decoding skills. Chapter 2 of *ParaReading* training will prepare you to use the instructional materials that are provided. Knowing the sounds of the letters and letter combinations and the ways to help students learn and recall those sounds are important skills for you to have.

LETRS

Chapter 2: Phonics Discussion

Phonics, also called decoding, is a critical skill. Children who become proficient decoders become proficient readers!

Learn the difference:

Phonemes = *sounds*.

Phonics = how the sounds are represented by *letters*.

Your Turn to Learn

A good place to start when preparing to teach phonics skills is with a review of the individual sound-symbol relationships most common in our written language. As a tutor, you must:

♦ Demonstrate proficiency with the most common sound-symbol relationships.

♦ Use a multisensory teaching approach when decoding words.

♦ Work with instructional materials to teach phonics.

Phonemes are the *sounds* of our language; graphemes are the *written letters or groups of letters* that represent the phonemes. Phonemes are the spoken elements, and graphemes are the written symbols for phonemes. When we teach *phonemic awareness*, we ask students to provide *sounds*; when we teach *phonics*, we ask students to match *letters* to the sounds. Each is an aspect of language. Phonemic awareness is spoken language, but phonics requires the visual recognition of letters and letter patterns.

Tutors Know! Phonemes are the sounds, and Phonics adds the letters! *Phonemes* = oral language. *Phonics* = oral language plus letters!

With phonics, we teach children to match letters to sounds:

Exercise #7: Phonemic Awareness or Phonics: Which One Is It?

Follow your trainer's directions to create phonics and phonemic awareness response cards for this activity. Listen to the sample teaching prompts. Determine if the students are being asked to use phonemic awareness or phonics, and hold up either the **Phonemic Awareness** or the **Phonics** card to show which focus skill is called for.

1. How many sounds in *bat*?

2. Sound out this written word: *rug*.

3. What silent letter is at the end of *game*?

4. What letter makes the sound "/s/"?

5. "/f/ /r/ /o/ /g/" What word?

6. Spell the longest word you know.

7. Tell me the middle sound in *mom*.

8. Tap the sounds in *lake*.

9. Find another word that ends with an -*m*.

10. Say *bed* without "/b/."

11. What two letters say "/sh/."

12. Spell the first syllable in *cracker*.

13. Change the /ŏ/ in cop to /ă/. What's the word?

Review and Practice: Phonics

Exercise #8: Making Grapheme Tiles

Welcome to the Grid! Use Grid One (a reproducible copy is available at the end of the workbook) to record the graphemes with their associated sounds as your trainer presents them. Each sound is presented with a key word that will help you recall the correct pronunciation of the letter sound.

When you are finished, practice saying the sounds randomly with a partner. Take turns, point to the letters, and randomly ask your partner to say the sounds for the graphemes. Help each other. Your trainer will come around and check for accuracy.

Tutors Know! *Grapheme*: The letter or letters that are used to represent and spell one sound. *–igh* is a grapheme for /ie/, and *–ea* is a grapheme for /ee/.

Exercise #9: Making Pairs of Words

Cut out the letter tiles in Grid Two (a reproducible copy is available at the end of the workbook). or write the letters on post it notes. Arrange the graphemes in front of you as directed by your trainer.

Single vowel spellings: o, u, i   **Consonants:** n, b, g, l, s, m, p

Digraphs: th, ng, sh   **Vowel spellings:** aw, oo, ur, ee

Create the following groups of letter tiles, and follow your trainer's directions to practice decoding using "minimal" pairs of words—words that differ by only one sound! Record the words you make for later reference. Have fun!

Set One: o, u, g, m, s, l, b

_____

Set Two: oo, i, ur, aw, l, s, n, p

_____

Set Three: o, i, ee, ng, th, s, l, n, sh

_____

Grid One

Grid Two

o	u	i	a			
n	b	g	l	s	m	p
th	ng	sh				
aw	oo	ur	ee			
f	t					
r	c					

Nonsense Words

When we want to check a student's ability to sound out words, to decode, we give them nonsense words. These are "make-believe" words that give us a sense of how well students are able to figure out unfamiliar *real* words when they come across them in their reading. Listen and follow along while your trainer decodes the following nonsense words.

vog	tel	ut
zek	zub	pef
trum	blesh	splin
gake	pune	lete
tark	yort	mir
soik	zail	shay
quawp	woam	prew

Exercise #10

Take turns with your partner and decode these same words. You will be asked to read a *new* set of nonsense words to your trainer during the review.

How to Teach It: Phonics

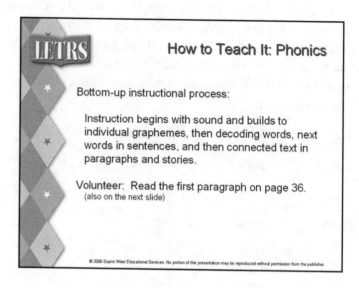

Most remedial reading lessons teach phonics skills from the "bottom up." This means that the lesson begins with the phonic elements and builds to a syllable or word. For example, to teach the digraph *sh*, the sound /sh/ is introduced. The grapheme is presented, then single words with *sh* are provided for practice. The words are presented in sentences, then paragraphs. This provides students with teacher support during the initial stages of learning a new concept and the gradual ascent to independent reading. It also gives students ample opportunity to practice the new skill.

The di<u>sh</u> was full of <u>sh</u>iny shells. The <u>sh</u>rimp did not <u>sh</u>ed their <u>sh</u>ells, so there were no <u>sh</u>rimp <u>sh</u>ells to <u>sh</u>ow them.	paragraph
The <u>sh</u>ip went to find big <u>sh</u>ells under the water.	sentence
<u>sh</u>ip, di<u>sh</u>	words
<u>sh</u> written	grapheme
/sh/	sound

Tutors Know! Much of a paraeducator's teaching responsibility is to provide the important *review* and *practice* that students at risk desperately need to strengthen and build their reading skills. *Review* means that information introduced at an earlier time is revisited. *Practice* means that additional time is spent applying and using the new skills.

Teaching Individual Letter Sounds

Before the strategies for teaching decoding *words* are introduced, it is important to discuss the student who is at the very early stages of decoding and just learning the *sounds* for individual letters. This student will require drill and practice to begin connecting the sounds to letters before blending them into words. To assist with this process, the teacher presents the letters and provides the sounds that are associated with the letters. Moveable letters provide a great tool for teaching the early stages of decoding.

Tutors Know! *Movable Letters* (*Letter Tiles*) are a tool that increases a child's interaction with the process of decoding and spelling. Movable letters may be actual letter shapes or letters printed on squares of paper.

Exercise #11
Find the following graphemes that you cut from Grid Two:

m	s	f	t	a

Role-play with your trainer. You will be the student, and your trainer will be the tutor. Follow the directions with your moveable letters to experience how to teach letter sounds.

Procedure for Teaching Letter Sounds:

1. "This letter *m* makes the sound /m/. Say it with me, /m/. What sound does the *m* (pointing) make?" "When we see *m* in a word, we say /m/."

   Follow the same process for each letter, teaching the sounds.

2. Point randomly to the letters, asking for the sounds. Point and say, "What sound?" Keep a quick pace. Make it lively: "I am going to try to trick you…"

3. Ask the student to show you a given sound. "Show me the /s/. Show me the /ă/."

Exercise #12

Pair up and role-play student and tutor. Use the following grapheme tiles:

| p | n | r | c | o |

Practice the previous steps for introducing and practicing the individual letter sounds.

Teach the letter sounds and then ask two types of questions to provide extra practice:

♦ "Show me the /_ / sound."

♦ Pointing to a letter: "What sound is this?"

Procedures For Teaching Blending

This section outlines four procedures that you can use to teach decoding and blending skills:

1. Whole-Word Blending

2. Stretch-and-Say Blending

3. Tap and Blend

4. Sounds to Spelling—This method uses the *encoding* or spelling process as a way of practicing and recalling the graphemes that are used to represent sounds.

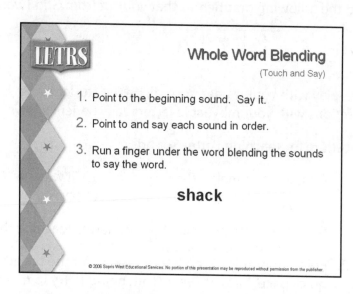

LETRS

Whole Word Blending
(Touch and Say)

1. Point to the beginning sound. Say it.

2. Point to and say each sound in order.

3. Run a finger under the word blending the sounds to say the word.

shack

© 2006 Sopris West Educational Services. No portion of this presentation may be reproduced without permission from the publisher.

Whole-Word Blending

Another name for this procedure is "touch and say." Children touch each letter (or grapheme), say the sounds, and then blend the sounds to read the word.

Step-by-step procedure for decoding *shack*:

1. Point to the digraph *sh* at the beginning of *shack*. Say "sound"; students say "/sh/."

2. Touch each successive grapheme, saying "sound" for each one, /sh/ /a/ /k/, as the children make the sound that each grapheme stands for. Then go back and blend the whole word smoothly, running your finger under the word, left to right, at the rate of about one phoneme each half second.

    Continuous sounds are easier to begin with. For example, *bat* (/b/ /a/ /t/) and *check* (/ch/ /e/ /ck/) are a little harder than *shell*, *thin*, or *moss*.

3. Slowly compress the extended word. Go from *shshshaaack* to *shshaack* to *shack*.

4. Point to the word and say, "The word is *shack*."

5. Check for understanding of the word and the ability to use it in a sentence.

Role-play Whole-Word Blending with your trainer.

LETRS

Whole Word Blending

Role play with your trainer. Practice with these words:

sand

fox

bath

© 2006 Sopris West Educational Services. No portion of this presentation may be reproduced without permission from the publisher.

Stretch-and-Say Blending

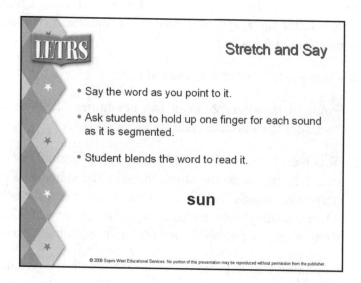

Phonemes are segmented and counted and then the whole word is blended with an accompanying gesture to pull the sounds together into the word.

Step-by-step procedure for decoding *sun*:

1. Say the whole word, "Sun."

2. Ask students to hold up one finger for each sound they hear as the word is segmented and the phonemes counted.

3. Say the whole word while pulling your arm down or sweeping it across your body from left to right.

Role-play Stretch-and-Say Blending with your trainer.

Tap and Blend

This method is similar to Whole-Word Blending except that the student is actively involved with the decoding process through *tapping* the sounds as tutor and student work through the word together.

Step-by-step procedure for decoding *stick*:

In unison, tutor and student tap index finger and thumb together as they say each sound in the word and blend the sounds together. If needed, the tutor can touch each grapheme as the student taps the sounds.

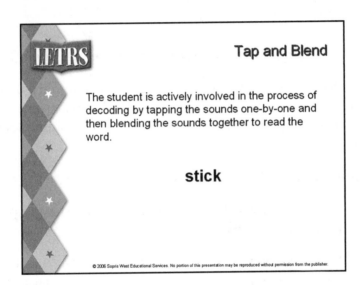

1. Tap and say "/s/."

2. Tap and say "/t/."

3. Tap and say "/ĭ/."

4. Tap and say "/k/."

5. Run finger under whole word and say, "Stick."

Tap and Blend adds a multisensory element that assists the student with connecting the individual sounds with the letters in words. As with any decoding method, children progress from oral decoding of words to silent decoding. Some students need more time to decode orally before transitioning to silent decoding and then to automatic decoding of unfamiliar words.

Role-play Tap and Blend with your trainer.

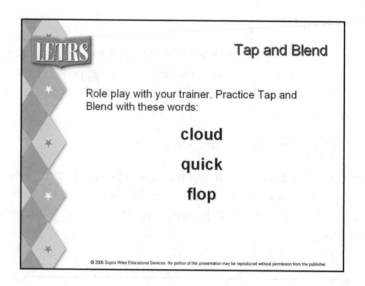

Sounds to Spelling—Phoneme Grapheme Mapping (Grace, 2007)

This method adds another very closely related skill to the decoding process: encoding. The student separates the sounds in a word and applies the grapheme for those sounds. That is, the student *spells* the word.

You will need the following materials:

♦ Copies of the Sounds to Spelling form or a sheet of paper with boxes and lines.

♦ Moveable sound markers—paper squares or little crackers, some small items that the students can use to represent the separate phonemes.

♦ Carefully chosen words from the student's reading materials.

Step-by-step procedure for decoding *book*:

1. Tutor says, "Book."

2. Student repeats the word and moves markers into boxes for each separate sound, saying the sounds as the markers are touched and moved—"/b/ /ŏo/ /k/."

3. The tutor asks two types of questions about the sounds: "Show me the /k/," and then, pointing to the second sound marker, "What is this sound?" Student says, "/ŏo/." These two questions can be repeated for different sounds in the word so that the student is responding to questions about all of the represented sounds.

4. Once the questions have been asked, the student is instructed to push up the markers one at a time and write the graphemes for each sound in the spaces, saying the sounds as the letters are written.

5. The student then writes the entire word on the line.

Role-play Sounds to Spelling with your trainer. Use the Sounds to Spelling form; a reproducible copy is available at the end of the workbook.

LETRS

Sounds to Spelling

Practice Sounds to Spelling with your trainer using these words:

shop

sand

shirt

© 2006 Sopris West Educational Services. No portion of this presentation may be reproduced without permission from the publisher.

Tutors Know! **Decoding:** given a *written* word, sounding it out to *read* it. **Encoding:** given a *spoken* word, sounding it out to *write* it!

Sounds to Spelling

Student Name: _____

Practice It: Phonics

The use of moveable letters to teach letter-sound correspondence and four instructional strategies for decoding whole words were introduced in the previous section. Now it is time for you to practice using these strategies to begin building confidence and automaticity with their use. Additional practice with children is recommended. The following role-playing activities are designed to provide experience with each of the four strategies. Practice the Error Response procedure when the "student" makes errors. Record data as instructed on the data form provided.

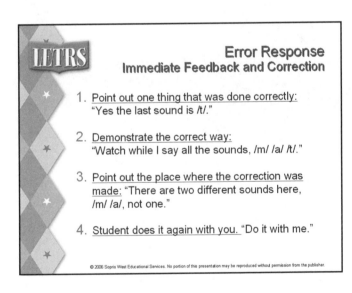

Error Response

1. Point out one part that was done correctly. "This first sound is /s/; you were right!"

2. Demonstrate the correct way. "Watch and listen while I do it." Decode each sound correctly, and blend the sounds to say the word.

3. Point out the place where a correction was made. "This middle sound here (pointing) is /ŏ/; I heard you say /ŭ/. What sound will you say next time?"

4. Student does it again with you. "Do it correctly with me."

Exercise #13: Individual Letter Sounds

Pair up and take turns as student and tutor to role-play the steps for introducing and practicing individual letter sounds. When you role-play the student, make a few errors to give your partner practice with the error-response process.

- ◆ Tutor #1 uses the following letter squares: p, n, r, c, o.

- ◆ Tutor #2 uses the following letter squares: d, h, k, l, i.

Directions:

1. "This letter *m* makes the sound /m/. Say it with me, /m/. What sound does the *m* (pointing) make?" "When we see *m* in a word, we say /m/."

   Follow the same process for each letter, teaching the sounds.

2. Point randomly to the letters, asking for the sounds. Point and say, "What sound?" Keep a quick pace. Make it lively: "I am going to try to trick you…."

3. Ask the student to show you a given sound. "Show me the /s/. Show me the /ă/."

Data Recording

Provide recording data during your role-playing practice.

1. Student does this well:

2. Student errors:

3. Sound confusion?

Exercise #14: Whole-Word Blending

Pair up and practice the steps for Whole-Word Blending. When you role-play the student, make a few errors to give your partner practice with the error-response process.

Please note that /ar/, /ou/, and /ee/ stand for single vowel sounds.

♦ Tutor #1 uses the following words: *crash, swim, steep*.

♦ Tutor #2 uses the following words: *brush, star, trout*.

Example—Whole-Word Blending

Step-by-step procedure for decoding *shack*:

1. Point to the digraph *sh* and say "Sound"; students say "/sh/."

2. Point to the *a* and say "Sound"; students say "/ă/."

3. Point to the *ck* and say "Sound"; students say "/k/."

4. Slide fingers under the whole word to blend it; students say "Shack."

5. Point to the word and say, "The word is *shack*."

6. Check for understanding and the ability to use the word in a sentence.

Data Recording

Provide words when discussing errors.

1. Student does this well:

2. Student errors:

3. Sound confusion?

Exercise #15: Stretch-and-Say Blending

Pair up and role-play the steps for introducing and practicing Stretch-and-Say Blending. When you role-play the student, make a few errors to give your partner practice with the error-response process.

- ◆ Tutor #1 uses the following words: *pine, tape, glue.*

- ◆ Tutor #2 uses the following words: *game, home, bike.*

Example—Stretch-and-Say Blending

Step-by-step procedure for decoding *sun*:

1   Say the whole word, "Sun."

2   Ask students to hold up one finger for each sound they hear as the word is segmented and the phonemes counted.

3   Say the whole word while pulling your arm down or sweeping it across your body from left to right.

Data Recording

Provide words when discussing errors.

1.   Student does this well:

2.   Student errors:

3.   Sound confusion?

Exercise #16: Tap and Blend

Pair up and role-play the steps for introducing and practicing Tap and Blend. When you role-play the student, make a few errors to give your partner practice with the error-response process.

♦ Tutor #1 uses the following words: *lunch, harsh, turn.*

♦ Tutor #2 uses the following words: *tooth, clay, boots.*

Example—Tap and Blend

Step-by-step procedure for decoding *stick*:

In unison, the teacher and student tap index finger and thumb together as they say each sound in the word and blend the sounds together. If needed, the teacher can touch each grapheme as the student taps the sounds.

1. Tap and say "/s/."

2. Tap and say "/t/."

3. Tap and say "/i/."

4. Tap and say "/k/."

5. Run finger under whole word and say, "Stick."

Data Recording

Provide words when discussing errors.

1. Student does this well:

2. Student errors:

3. Sound confusion?

Exercise #17: Sounds to Spelling

Pair up and role-play the steps for practicing Sounds to Spelling using the Sounds to Spelling form. When you role-play the student, make a few errors to give your partner practice with the error-response process.

- ◆ Tutor #1 uses the following words: *bricks, farming, paint.*

- ◆ Tutor #2 uses the following words: *white, thirsty, healing.*

Example—Sounds to Spelling

Step-by-step procedure for decoding *book*:

1. Tutor says, "Book."

2. Student repeats the word and moves markers into the spaces for each separate sound, saying the sounds as the markers are touched and moved—"/b/ /ŏŏ/ /k/."

3. The tutor asks two types of questions about the sounds: "Show me the /k/," and then, pointing to the second sound marker, "What is this sound?" Student says, "/ŏŏ/." These two questions can be repeated for different sounds in the word so that the student is responding to questions about all of the represented sounds.

4. Once the questions have been asked, the student is instructed to push up the markers one at a time and write the graphemes for each sound in the spaces, saying the sounds as the letters are written.

5. The student then writes the entire word on the line.

Data Recording

Provide words when discussing errors.

1. Student does this well:

2. Student errors:

3. Sound confusion?

Moving From One Syllable to Two

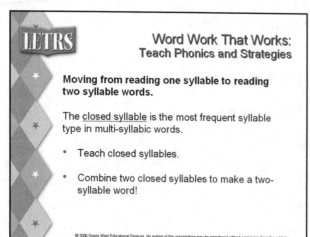

Word Work That Works:
Teach Phonics and Strategies

Moving from reading one syllable to reading two syllable words.

The closed syllable is the most frequent syllable type in multi-syllabic words.

- Teach closed syllables.

- Combine two closed syllables to make a two-syllable word!

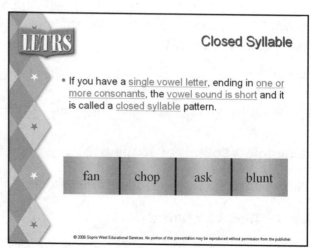

Closed Syllable

- If you have a single vowel letter, ending in one or more consonants, the vowel sound is short and it is called a closed syllable pattern.

| fan | chop | ask | blunt |

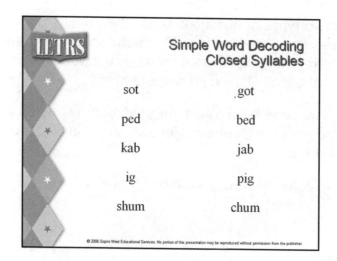

Simple Word Decoding
Closed Syllables

sot	got
ped	bed
kab	jab
ig	pig
shum	chum

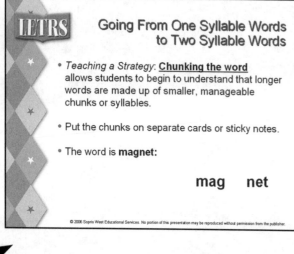

Going From One Syllable Words
to Two Syllable Words

- *Teaching a Strategy*: **Chunking the word** allows students to begin to understand that longer words are made up of smaller, manageable chunks or syllables.

- Put the chunks on separate cards or sticky notes.

- The word is **magnet**:

mag   net

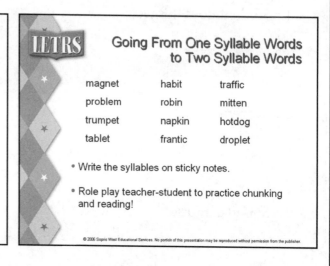

Going From One Syllable Words
to Two Syllable Words

magnet	habit	traffic
problem	robin	mitten
trumpet	napkin	hotdog
tablet	frantic	droplet

- Write the syllables on sticky notes.

- Role play teacher-student to practice chunking and reading!

Review: Phonics

1. What skill is practiced in Chapter 2? _____

2. Name and describe two blending processes used to teach decoding in Chapter 2. _____

    _____

    _____

    _____

    _____

    _____

3. What is the benefit of recording a student's performance when decoding? _____

    _____

    _____

    _____

    _____

    _____

4. Describe the steps for responding to student errors. _____

    _____

    _____

    _____

    _____

    _____

5. Be ready to decode a selection of nonsense words for the trainer.

Chapter 3: Fluency

Discussion

The ultimate goal of reading instruction is for students to be automatic with the skills they use to read. Just like learning to play a musical instrument or ride a bicycle, there are underlying reading skills that, with practice and time, reach a level of ease that allows the process to happen effortlessly. Reaching this level of fluency isn't always easy. When students read fluently, they have automaticity with other reading skills: phonemic awareness, decoding, and word recognition. When a student is a fluent reader, the demanding tasks of decoding are automatic, and energy expended during the reading process can be directed to comprehension of the material that is being read. This is the ultimate goal for our students: to become fluent readers able to gain meaning from the written word, apply higher-order thinking skills, infer meaning, and expand their knowledge of the world from reading.

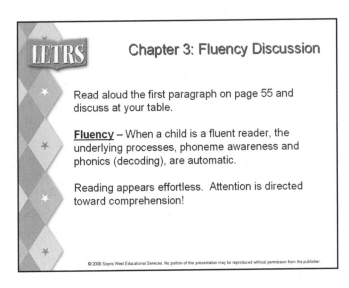

LETRS

Chapter 3: Fluency Discussion

Read aloud the first paragraph on page 55 and discuss at your table.

Fluency – When a child is a fluent reader, the underlying processes, phoneme awareness and phonics (decoding), are automatic.

Reading appears effortless. Attention is directed toward comprehension!

© 2006 Sopris West Educational Services. No portion of this presentation may be reproduced without permission from the publisher.

The first two chapters in *ParaReading* taught us about phonemic awareness through sound segmentation and blending, and applying letters to sounds through phonics and spelling. Chapter 3 builds on this instruction and focuses on working with students to build *automaticity* with these skills so that students can develop fluent reading habits. Previous studies have shown that trained tutors play an important role with helping young readers to significantly improve reading fluency (Glaser, 2002).

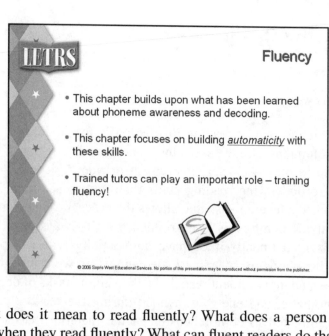

What does it mean to read fluently? What does a person sound like when they read fluently? What can fluent readers do that non-fluent readers are unable to do? These questions will be answered in this chapter.

Your Turn to Learn

Listen to your trainer simulate two different students reading. Answer these questions:

♦ What does a fluent reader sound like?

♦ What does a disfluent reader sound like?

♦ What do you think are the advantages of being able to read fluently?

How do students become fluent readers? Many become fluent readers from lots of practice with reading, similar to the practice that is commonly prescribed to improve musical or athletic performance. Repeated skill practice improves the performance of a skill. To improve reading fluency for many students at risk, it takes reading practice plus additional *fluency training*. Fluency training is the instructional focus of Chapter 3. But first, let's look at the processes involved in the task of reading fluently.

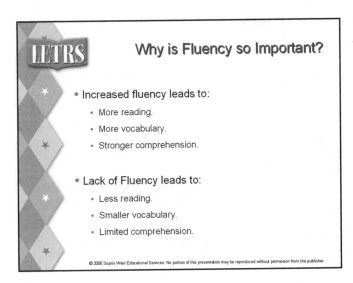

Eye-Voice Span

Eye-voice span enables us to move our eyes ahead of our voice when we read. Your trainer will lead you through an activity that will provide you with an opportunity to experience eye-voice span.

What do you notice when the projected image is removed from sight? The trainer is able to continue reading a few words even after the image disappears! This ability is characteristic of fluent readers. When the reading process is automatic, our conscious attention is focused on meaning, and our eyes move ahead of our voice.

Helping students become fluent readers begins with teaching phonemic awareness and decoding skills. A firm grounding with these skills allows them to read isolated words and build automaticity with sight recognition. The frequent reading of connected text, sentences, and stories helps young students become fluent. Many students require special attention to reach levels of fluency that will allow them to progress with their reading skills. The common instructional process is to have the student read material several times until they attain fluency with the material. This practice is called *repeated readings*.

Repeated readings provide fluency training with:

♦ Letter decoding

♦ Single-word decoding

♦ Reading connected text

Repeated Readings

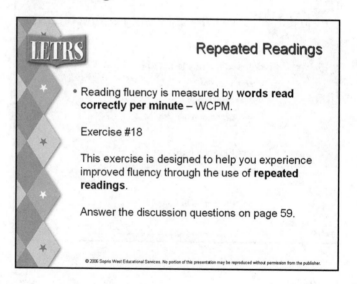

Fluency has been a focus of key reading research over the past several years. Reading fluency is measured by words read correctly per minute (WCPM) during the reading of instructional level material over three consecutive readings of the same material. The following activity has been prepared to provide an opportunity for you to experience the process and effects of repeated readings.

Exercise #18: Building Fluency with the Unfamiliar

Your trainer will take you through an exercise designed to help you experience improved fluency through the use of repeated readings. It is impossible for an adult to entirely duplicate the experience of a young child, but this practice comes close. During the process, pay attention to your responses, observations, and any questions that arise. Jot them down for discussion.

1. What were your initial reactions to the text? _____

_____

_____

_____

_____

_____

_____

_____

_____

_____

2. What are your observations with each successive reading? _____

_____

_____

_____

_____

_____

_____

_____

_____

3. Did your initial responses to the text change with exposure through repeated readings? How? _____

_____

_____

_____

_____

_____

_____

_____

How to Teach It: Fluency

The step-by-step process for using **repeated readings** is outlined in this section and can be used with students from a variety of reading levels. Repeated readings can be used to build fluency with individual letter sounds, isolated words, and with reading passages.

> **Tutors Know!** *Isolated words* means that words are presented alone, separate from connected or story text. A word list provides isolated words.

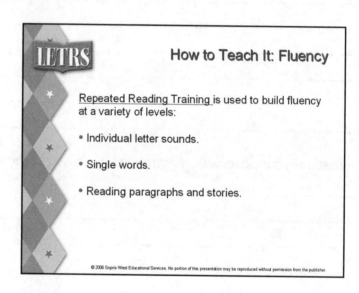

LETRS

How to Teach It: Fluency

Repeated Reading Training is used to build fluency at a variety of levels:

- Individual letter sounds.

- Single words.

- Reading paragraphs and stories.

© 2006 Sopris West Educational Services. No portion of this presentation may be reproduced without permission from the publisher.

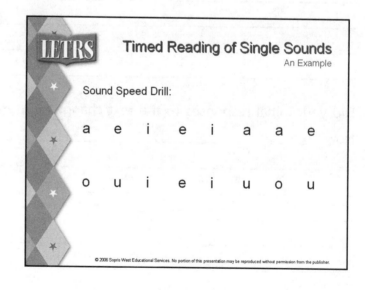

LETRS

Timed Reading of Single Sounds
An Example

Sound Speed Drill:

a　e　i　e　i　a　a　e

o　u　i　e　i　u　o　u

© 2006 Sopris West Educational Services. No portion of this presentation may be reproduced without permission from the publisher.

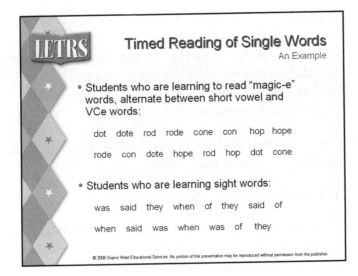

♦ If your students are just beginning to learn **letter sounds**, repeated readings are to be done with a page of letters from which letter sounds will be read.

♦ If your students are **decoding and blending single words** to practice building automaticity, do repeated readings with isolated words that reflect the target decoding skills.

♦ Once your students are reading **passages of text such as paragraphs and stories**, use these texts for repeated readings. This level of repeated reading generally begins around mid-first grade.

Materials You Will Need to Do the Repeated Readings:

Stories and Paragraphs: Repeated Readings

- Use reading material that is at the student's instructional level (90-95% accuracy).
- Copy of the page student is reading.
- Stopwatch.
- Three colored markers or colored pencils.
- Repeated Readings Fluency Chart.

© 2006 Sopris West Educational Services. No portion of this presentation may be reproduced without permission from the publisher.

◆ *Reading material that is written at an instructional level for your student.* This can be had in many ways: 1) Ask the classroom teacher to recommend appropriate reading material; 2) Use the classroom reading curriculum; 3) Use reading fluency training passages that are grade leveled and provide counted words for you.

◆ *A copy of the page the student will be reading.* You will use this to record student errors.

◆ *A stopwatch.* This is a necessary tool.

◆ *Three colored markers or colored pencils to record the errors.* Use one color for each reading to visually separate the errors in the first, second, and third readings.

◆ *A copy of the Fluency Training: Repeated Readings Chart.* A reproducible version is available at the end of the workbook.

Repeated Readings

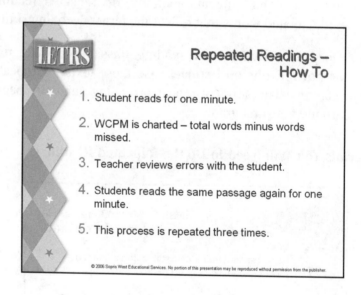

LETRS

Repeated Readings –
How To

1. Student reads for one minute.

2. WCPM is charted – total words minus words missed.

3. Teacher reviews errors with the student.

4. Students reads the same passage again for one minute.

5. This process is repeated three times.

© 2006 Sopris West Educational Services. No portion of this presentation may be reproduced without permission from the publisher.

Step-by-Step Process

Instruct the student: "Please read this passage for your fluency training today. Begin reading here (point), and read until I tell you to stop. If you come to a word you don't know, I will tell you the word." Time him for one minute, and note the number of words he reads. Subtract the errors for a total of words correct per minute (WCPM).

1. Chart the WCPM on the Fluency Training: Repeated Readings Chart. Show the student how to graph his own performance.

2. Review the errors with the student. Show and tell him the words you helped him with, words he omitted or substituted, and words he hesitated with.

3. Instruct the student to read the passage again, and follow the same procedure.

4. Do this for a total of three times, marking the errors with a different color each time. Have the student graph his performance after each reading. Work with the student to set goals between readings—"How many words can you read next time? Can you beat your time?"

Tutors Know! *WCPM* means "words read correctly per minute." The total number of words that a student correctly reads in one minute is that student's WCPM.

Reading Errors

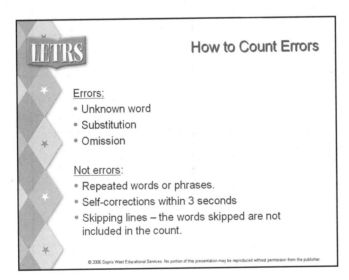

When you do repeated readings, you will also need to know what to count as a reading error. The following guidelines tell you what to count as a reading error:

♦ *Unknown word.* The student hesitates or attempts to read a word but does not produce the correct word in three seconds. Provide the correct word for the student and mark it as an error on your sheet.

Fluency Training: Repeated Readings Chart

Student Name: _____

	Date: _____ Reading Selection: _____ _____	Date: _____ Reading Selection: _____ _____	Date: _____ Reading Selection: _____ _____	

Words Read Correctly Per Minute

120												120
100												100
90												90
80												80
70												70
60												60
50												50
40												40
30												30
20												20
10												10
0												0
	1	2	3		1	2	3		1	2	3	

♦ *Substitution*. The student misreads a word, substituting a different word for the actual word in the text.

♦ *Omission*. The student leaves a word out while reading.

Do not count as errors:

♦ Rereading words or phrases

♦ Self-corrections made within three seconds

♦ Skipping a line (Do not count the words in the omitted line as errors.)

Exercise #19

There are several steps to follow when using repeated readings to improve reading fluency. Your trainer will now take you through each of the repeated readings steps with sample text. Review what to count as *reading errors* with a partner prior to going through the process, and then practice the process. Use the text and repeated readings chart provided.

Listen to your trainer read this passage three times. Follow along during the three separate readings, and note errors. Record the WCPM after each reading. Be ready to discuss your experiences.

(continued) **Exercise #19**

All About Plants

There are many plants on our earth. Plants can be big. Plants can be	14
small. We can't even see some plants. They are too small. Plants need many	28
things to grow. They need sunlight. Some plants need a lot of sunlight.	41
Others need very little sunlight. Plants need water to grow. Just like	54
sunlight, some plants need a lot of water. Other plants need very little	67
water. A cactus can live without a lot of water.	77
Plants also need food from the soil to grow. Plants use their roots to	91
get food and water from the soil. The roots also hold up the plant. The	106
leaves make food for the plant. They use the sun to make food. Stems are	121
different on plants. The stems hold up the leaves and flowers on the plant. It	136
also carries water and food to the plant. The stem of a tree is hard and	152
strong. The stem of a flower can bend easily. Plants have seeds to grow new	167
plants. Some seeds are very small. Other seeds are in fruit that grows on the	182
plants. Some plants have flowers. Other plants do not have flowers. Plants	194
give us many things. They are good to us.	203

Words Read Correctly Per Minute			
100			
90			
80			
70			
60			
50			
40			
30			
20			
10			
0			
	1	2	3

Adapted by permission of the publisher from Gail Adams and Sheron Brown, *Six-Minute Solution: A Reading Fluency Program* (Longmont, CO: Sopris West, 2004), p. 40, © 2004 by Sopris West.

Practice It: Fluency

Exercise #20

Form small groups of three or four. Use the sample re-peated readings practice pages to practice repeated readings. There is one example for each of the three levels of beginning reader: letter sounds, isolated words, and connected text.

- ◆ Listen to the trainer simulate a child's timed performance.

- ◆ Record errors on the text as you listen.

- ◆ Record WCPM on the chart at the close of each minute's reading.

- ◆ Discuss, compare errors, analysis, and data recording with the other members of your group before the next reading.

(continued) **Exercise #20**

Repeated Readings Sample 1: Letter Sounds

Say the letter sounds.

i	th	g	l	s	b	h	g	w	sh	a	u	12
h	f	x	e	a	ch	p	n	t	o	v	m	24
p	qu	s	y	n	c	d	j	r	sh	d	y	36
b	e	th	z	m	k	l	x	a	n	i	p	48
r	ch	s	y	t	th	qu	f	v	g	d	e	60

Number of Sounds Read Correctly

	1	2	3
100			
90			
80			
70			
60			
50			
40			
30			
20			
10			
0			

(continued) **Exercise #20**

Repeated Readings Sample 2: Isolated Words

fed	cut	fed	kid	then	pan	6
net	path	wet	fad	rut	lop	12
then	wet	kip	dub	that	fat	18
rug	that	bag	peg	rug	let	24
pen	bath	than	fed	did	log	30
thin	dad	fad	thin	bath	fell	36
bib	this	peg	path	pen	that	42
rut	kid	keg	net	get	pill	48
did	that	jam	bib	dad	dug	54
get	gum	kit	wet	cut	lid	60

Number of Sounds Read Correctly

	1	2	3
100			
90			
80			
70			
60			
50			
40			
30			
20			
10			
0			

(continued) **Exercise #20**

A History of Flight: Hot Air Balloons

For thousands of years, people dreamed of traveling in the air like birds. The only 15
problem was, people had no way to fly. Then, about two hundred years ago, two French 31
brothers made a big balloon. They lit a small fire under the balloon and watched as the 49
balloon rose in the air. Their balloon was flying! 57

Would you like to understand how the hot air balloon could fly? Hot air is lighter 73
than cold air. When the brothers lit the fire, as the air got hotter, it got lighter, and the 92
balloon began to fly. What do you think happened when the air in the balloon got cold? 109

The brothers put a rooster, a sheep, and a duck on the first flight of their balloon. 126
Before long, many people rode in hot air balloons. 135

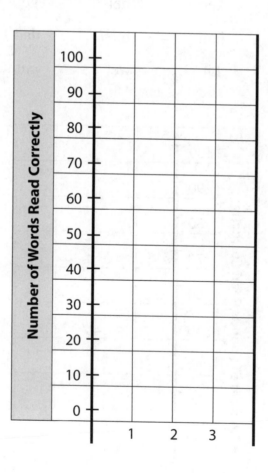

Review: Fluency

1. Why is reading fluency a critical skill for students to improve? _____
_____
_____
_____
_____
_____
_____

2. What process do effective tutors use to help students improve reading fluency? Explain.
_____
_____
_____
_____
_____
_____

3. What will you count as errors during repeated readings? _____
_____
_____

4. What does not constitute an error? _____
_____
_____

5. List, in order, the first three skills that have been introduced in *ParaReading* and an example of
   how to teach each skill. _____
_____
_____
_____
_____
_____
_____
_____

Chapter 4: Vocabulary

Discussion

What does it mean to *know* a word? How do people learn the *meanings* of words? Why is *vocabulary* an important reading skill? These questions have been asked and studied by reading researchers for many years. We have learned that knowing a word's meaning helps us recognize the word when we see it in print. We know that first and second grade children need to learn more than 800 new words per year and older children need to learn 2000 to 3000 new words a year to be considered effective readers. Young children learn a substantial number of these words through hearing when stories and informational text are read to them. Older children learn most new words through reading themselves (Biemiller, 1999; Nagy & Anderson, 1984).

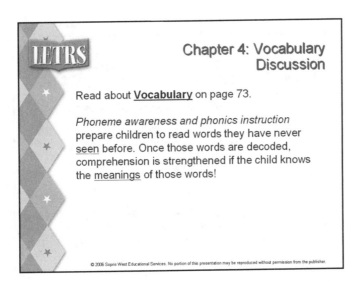

Chapter 4: Vocabulary Discussion

Read about **Vocabulary** on page 73.

Phoneme awareness and phonics instruction prepare children to read words they have never <u>seen</u> before. Once those words are decoded, comprehension is strengthened if the child knows the <u>meanings</u> of those words!

Even though young children can and should learn word meanings through listening to text (both narrative stories and expository or informational texts), listening can only supplement and not replace critical reading practice for older children. These children need exposure to vocabulary through reading in order to build a visual reference of words for future reading fluency.

Yet, the reality is that many children come to school from environments where they receive limited exposure to language and therefore have fewer opportunities to build the vocabulary that would improve their reading comprehension. These kids are behind from the start, and it is critical that schools provide many opportunities for them to increase their vocabulary knowledge.

Phonemic awareness and phonics instruction prepare children to figure out new words when they are reading. Once those words are decoded, comprehension of the text is strengthened if the child *knows the meanings of the words*. There are four major processors that work together to help us read and comprehend what we read, as shown on the diagram on the next page. This model also provides us with a basis from which to evaluate and plan instruction for students. The *orthographic processor* is the first to receive input from the printed page. This visual information is combined with a word's phonological information to decode words. Once a word is decoded, the *meaning processor* matches it with a known word, and its meaning is accessed. If the word is unknown, then comprehension is jeopardized. It is important to know that once a word's meaning is stored in the word-meaning area of the brain, it is more easily recognized in print (Adams, 1990). Increasing a student's vocabulary not only helps to develop word *recognition*, it also improves *comprehension*. All of the processors work together during the process of reading.

Exercise #21: Experience the Brain At Work

Use the items on the handout provided by your trainer and four-part processor model to learn more about how the brain processes information when we read. Place the pictures in the appropriate area to demonstrate which processor carries the load for the function given as your trainer takes you through a simulation of a child's reading and misplaced meaning!

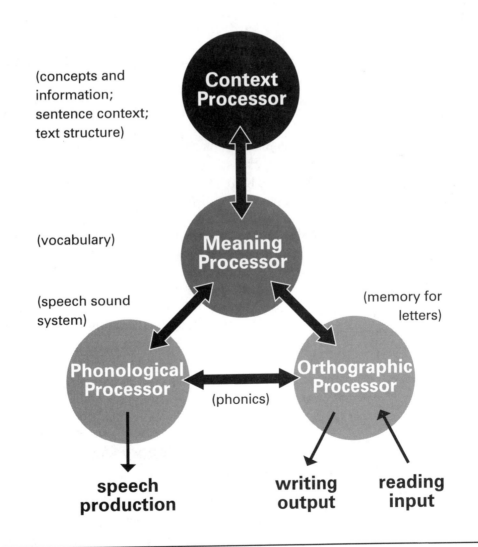

Your Turn to Learn

In this next section, you will participate in several exercises designed to increase your awareness of vocabulary and to prepare you to pay attention to vocabulary in your work with children. Are you ready? Here we go!

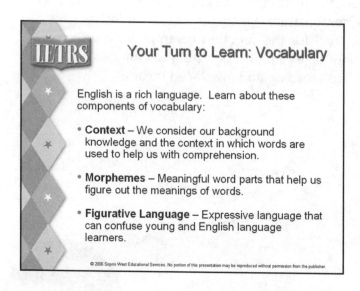

LETRS

Your Turn to Learn: Vocabulary

English is a rich language. Learn about these components of vocabulary:

- **Context** – We consider our background knowledge and the context in which words are used to help us with comprehension.

- **Morphemes** – Meaningful word parts that help us figure out the meanings of words.

- **Figurative Language** – Expressive language that can confuse young and English language learners.

Context, Morphemes, and Figurative Language

The English language is called a complex or "deep" language because it has several origins, which affect spelling and pronunciation and help us determine meanings of words. As a result of its hybrid nature, English is a rich language.

To determine the meanings of words, we use several approaches:

♦ We consider the *context* in which the word is used. For example, the word *bug* has an obvious meaning that comes to mind: a little insect. However, when presented in the following context the meaning changes: "Her little brother would *bug* her by sneaking up on her and pulling her braid." Or, " The detective placed a *bug* in the car so he could listen to the conversation while they were driving."

♦ We consider the meaningful word parts, or *morphemes*. For example, the meaning of the word "semicircle" can be determined when we know that semi means part or one-half.

♦ We combine information from our personal experience and context to interpret *figurative language*. For example, in the sentence, "Her *heart sank* when she saw that the lottery numbers did not match her selection," the person's heart does not really drop. The expression means that she was disappointed and saddened.

Context—Read the following passage. What do you think the underlined word means? What information in the context helps you figure it out?

> It was fortunate that the vendor had a box of <u>buckshee</u> for the children to choose from, because they did not have a single penny to spend. (Bryson, 1990, p. 237)

_____

_____

_____

_____

Morphemes—With a partner, brainstorm as many words as you can think of that have the word part *struc(t)*. Example: in<u>struc</u>tion.

_____

_____

_____

_____

Share your collection of words with your trainer.

Given the collection of words, can you guess the meaning of the morpheme *struc*? Discuss.

Figurative Language—Beautiful and interesting verbal expression is created through figurative language. It is a common tool used by authors to enrich content and individualize their writing. Adults may intuit the meaning of figurative language more easily than children. For this reason, it is important that teachers be aware of the use of figurative language in the text that children will be listening to or reading and prepare them for it. This is especially true with English-language learners.

Find the figurative language in each of the following examples. Work with your group to come up with explanations that you would provide for your students. Tip: Tie the figurative language to your own experience and help the children connect with a personal experience of their own.

My stomach flipped when I saw the cyclist approach the weakened wooden ramp at top speed.

_____

_____

_____

_____

It was a crisp autumn morning, and the sunlight transformed the reds, yellows, and oranges into a hillside sunrise.

_____

_____

_____

_____

How to Teach It: Vocabulary

As a paraeducator, you can help motivate students to learn new words. The approaches described below provide simple ways to help children build interest in words and increase their understanding and use of vocabulary. Enjoy being the student as your trainer models each of the *ParaReading* vocabulary teaching components.

LETRS

So many words
So little time!

Which words should be the focus of vocabulary instruction?

Vocabulary instruction should focus on words that the learner will find useful in many contexts.

National Reading Panel

Choice Vocabulary—Wonder Words

Wonder Words are words or phrases (figurative language) that you anticipate may present comprehension difficulty for your students. Prepare students by *preteaching* the Wonder Words to improve the students' text comprehension.

There are two components to *ParaReading* vocabulary instruction:

♦ You, the tutor, choose the Wonder Words and provide definitions.

♦ Students use a Wonder Words journal to log the words.

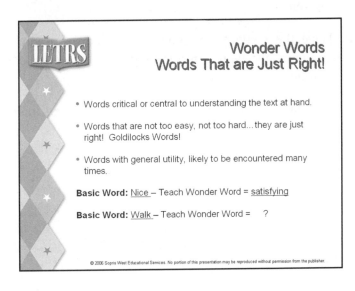

LETRS

Choosing Words to Teach
Bringing Words to Life
Beck, McKeown, Kucan, 2002

Tier 1: <u>Everyday Words</u> - these are easy words and generally are already known by most students.

Tier 2: <u>Extended Words</u> – the most useful words – these are words for which students have a concept and simpler vocabulary to define the word.

Tier 3: <u>Expert Words</u> – they are necessary for the story but may not come up often in conversation and other stories.

© 2006 Sopris West Educational Services. No portion of this presentation may be reproduced without permission from the publisher.

LETRS

Wonder Words
Words That are Just Right!

• Words critical or central to understanding the text at hand.

• Words that are not too easy, not too hard...they are just right! Goldilocks Words!

• Words with general utility, likely to be encountered many times.

Basic Word: <u>Nice</u> – Teach Wonder Word = <u>satisfying</u>

Basic Word: <u>Walk</u> – Teach Wonder Word = ?

© 2006 Sopris West Educational Services. No portion of this presentation may be reproduced without permission from the publisher.

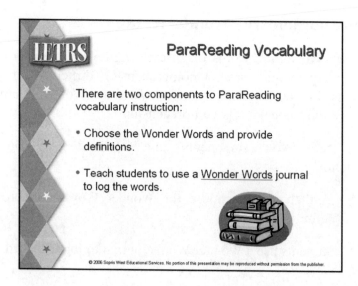

Vocabulary instruction begins with finding Wonder Words in material that you will be reading to the students or that they will be reading themselves. Follow these steps:

♦ Preread the material that your students will be reading or that you will read to your students.

♦ Choose two words that meet the Wonder Words criteria: a) words or phrases that may be difficult to understand and that the students may hear or read again and therefore need to know; or b) words that may have multiple meanings.

♦ Provide information about the words' definitions.

♦ Use each word or phrase in a sentence related to the reading selection.

♦ Have the students tell you a sentence using each word and enter the words into their Wonder Words vocabulary journals.

♦ Review the Wonder Words the next time you meet with your students.

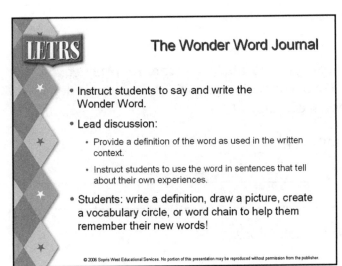

The Wonder Word Journal

- Instruct students to say and write the Wonder Word.

- Lead discussion:
  - Provide a definition of the word as used in the written context.
  - Instruct students to use the word in sentences that tell about their own experiences.

- Students: write a definition, draw a picture, create a vocabulary circle, or word chain to help them remember their new words!

© 2006 Sopris West Educational Services. No portion of this presentation may be reproduced without permission from the publisher.

Exercise #22

Now it's your turn to experience the *ParaReading* vocabulary lesson. Your trainer will take you through each of the steps in the lesson. Follow directions as each of the steps is demonstrated. Take notes to help you remember the lesson content.

1. Material is previewed and two words or phrases are chosen.

   _____

   _____

2. Provide information about the words' definitions.

   _____

   _____

3. Use the words in sentences related to the reading selection.

   _____

   _____

4. Have the students tell you a sentence using the word and enter the word into their Wonder Words journal.

   _____

   _____

Wonder Words Journal Page

_____

Vocabulary expansion occurs rapidly from birth through adolescence within communicative relationships. Everyday experiences with friends, caregivers, and community members shape speech habits and knowledge of language. The human mind latches onto new words as it hears them because they are the tools of communication. Humans have an intrinsic need to understand what is said to them and to share experience through language, and the brain is biologically adapted to support language acquisition. Before school and before learning to read, children learn most of the words they know through daily oral communication with adults. Adults facilitate that process when they introduce new words in a shared experience, elaborate what a child has said, confirm and clarify the child's attempts to use new words, deliberately repeat new words in conversation, or read aloud.

Reprinted by permission of the publisher from Louisa Moats, LETRS *Module 4* (Longmont CO: Sopris West, 2003), p. 9, ©2003 Sopris West Educational Services.

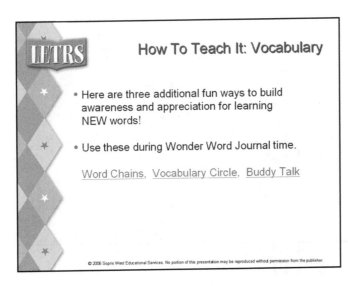

LETRS

How To Teach It: Vocabulary

- Here are three additional fun ways to build awareness and appreciation for learning NEW words!

- Use these during Wonder Word Journal time.

Word Chains, Vocabulary Circle, Buddy Talk

© 2006 Sopris West Educational Services. No portion of this presentation may be reproduced without permission from the publisher.

LETRS

Teach Word Relatives
Word Chains

- When we teach words in groups as *relatives*, it is easier for students to remember the words, retrieve the words, and use the words.

- These words are related in a meaning network: Connect, link, hook, latch, etc.

© 2006 Sopris West Educational Services. No portion of this presentation may be reproduced without permission from the publisher.

LETRS — Word Chains

Meaning Related:

doctor — physician — hospital — medication — ?

Morpheme Related:

direct — directly — indirect — ? — ?

© 2006 Sopris West Educational Services. No portion of this presentation may be reproduced without permission from the publisher.

LETRS — Word Chains: Activity

- Create a word chain with a partner.
- Share your word chains with a neighbor.

© 2006 Sopris West Educational Services. No portion of this presentation may be reproduced without permission from the publisher.

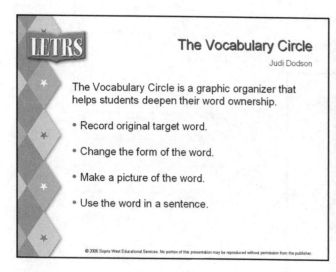

LETRS — The Vocabulary Circle

Judi Dodson

The Vocabulary Circle is a graphic organizer that helps students deepen their word ownership.

- Record original target word.
- Change the form of the word.
- Make a picture of the word.
- Use the word in a sentence.

© 2006 Sopris West Educational Services. No portion of this presentation may be reproduced without permission from the publisher.

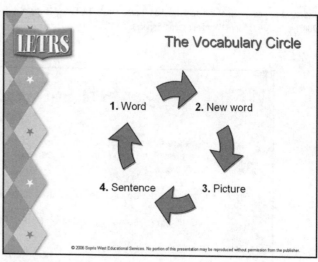

LETRS — The Vocabulary Circle

1. Word
2. New word
3. Picture
4. Sentence

© 2006 Sopris West Educational Services. No portion of this presentation may be reproduced without permission from the publisher.

LETRS — The Vocabulary Circle

Judi Dodson

1. music
2. musician
3.
4. The musician can really play that guitar!

Create a Vocabulary Circle with a partner.

© 2006 Sopris West Educational Services. No portion of this presentation may be reproduced without permission from the publisher.

LETRS — "Buddy Talk Activity"

Judi Dodson

Teachers prompt students to use Wonder Words.

Students use Wonder Words in conversation with each other, connecting it to their own experience.

Buddy talk with a partner. Use the word *intrinsic*.

© 2006 Sopris West Educational Services. No portion of this presentation may be reproduced without permission from the publisher.

"Giving the Gift of Repetition"

LETRS

Judi Dodson

- It takes multiple repetitions and exposures to words to develop word knowledge and ultimately word ownership.

- Teachers can use key words *intentionally* during instruction and throughout the day, to deepen word learning.

- It may take 12 repetitions for a student to own a word.

Brainstorm with a partner:
How will you "give the gift of repetition?".

© 2006 Sopris West Educational Services. No portion of this presentation may be reproduced without permission from the publisher.

Practice It: Vocabulary

Your turn to try it! Pair up with a partner; one of you will be Tutor #1, and the other will be Tutor #2. Read through your corresponding reading selection, and follow steps 1–4 to prepare for a vocabulary lesson.

Tutor #1

Beware of Bears

Bears! Many people are fascinated by them. After all, who can resist a stuffed, cuddly teddy bear? Bear enclosures at zoos are often a popular exhibit. Watching adorable bear cubs romp brings smiles and chuckles from onlookers.

Reprinted by permission of the publisher from Gail Adams and Sheron Brown, *Six-Minute Solution: A Reading Fluency Program* (Longmont, CO: Sopris West, 2004), p. 97, © 2004 by Sopris West.

1. Preread the material.

2. Choose two **Wonder Words** that may present difficulty in understanding:

_____   _____

3. Provide information about the words' definitions:

_____

_____

_____

4. Provide examples of the words' usages in context:

_____

_____

_____

_____

Data Recording—Record student performance and the Wonder Words you chose using the following form.

Vocabulary—(circle one) **Listening or Reading**

Can the student use the vocabulary words in a sentence that shows he/she knows the word?   Yes   No

What were the Wonder Words?

Tutor #2

Camels: One Hump or Two?

Camels are funny-looking animals with humps on their backs. Camels are large animals. They are seven or eight feet tall. They have small heads but long, curved necks. Their legs are long, but their bodies are heavy. Camels are used for riding or for carrying heavy loads.

Reprinted by permission of the publisher from Gail Adams and Sheron Brown, *Six-Minute Solution: A Reading Fluency Program* (Longmont, CO: Sopris West, 2004), p. 88, © 2004 by Sopris West.

1. Preread the mateial.

2. Choose two Wonder Words that may present difficulty in understanding:

   _____   _____

3. Provide information about the words' definitions:

   _____

   _____

   _____

4. Provide examples of the words' usages in context:

   _____

   _____

   _____

   _____

   _____

Data Recording—Record student performance and the Wonder Words you chose using the following form.

Vocabulary—(circle one) **Listening or Reading**

Can the student use the vocabulary words in a sentence that shows he/she knows the word?   Yes   No

What were the Wonder Words?

Now, #1 tutors get together, and #2 tutors get together. Compare your vocabulary choices and preparation. What are the similarities and differences? Why did you choose the words you did? Share your lesson preparations. What can we learn from each other?

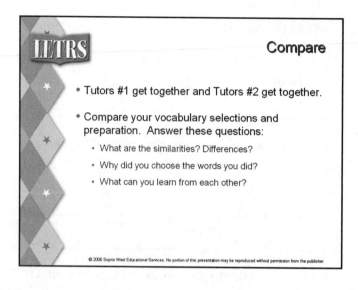

OK, get back together with your partner. One of you will act as the tutor and the other as the student. Use the following guidelines to practice *ParaReading* vocabulary instruction. The tutor first writes the chosen words on the Wonder Word journal page (a reproducible version is available at the end of the workbook), and then the "student" writes sentences using the words or draws pictures of the words. Switch roles when you have successfully completed your role-play.

1. Show the written Wonder Words to the student (journal page). Read the words. "These are Wonder Words that you will be reading today."

2. Read each word and provide definitions.

3. Tell about the word using the context of the story.

4. Have the student record a picture or brief definition in the Wonder Word journal to help recall the meaning.

5. Instruct the student to read the passage.

6. Record student performance using the data form.

Tip: Revisit the Wonder Words journal and discuss the words in relation to the story. Always encourage students to use the Wonder Words in their discussion. "Tell me about it, and use the word _____." Rephrase for the students if they do not use the Wonder Words. Provide opportunities for the students to apply the vocabulary to their own experiences.

Share role-play experiences with the whole group.

Wonder Words

Wonder Words

Review: Vocabulary

1. Describe the four-part processing system. Identify the four parts and tell how they work together to help gain meaning from written text. _____

   _____

   _____

   _____

   _____

   _____

   _____

   _____

   _____

2. Describe the process for choosing and defining the Wonder Words that you will teach your
   students. _____

   _____

   _____

   _____

   _____

   _____

   _____

   _____

   _____

3. Define *context*, and give an example of how it relates to teaching vocabulary. _____

   _____

   _____

   _____

   _____

   _____

   _____

   _____

4. Define *figurative language*, and tell how it relates to teaching vocabulary. _____

_____

_____

_____

_____

_____

_____

_____

_____

5. Define *morpheme*, and tell how morphemes relate to teaching and learning vocabulary.

_____

_____

_____

_____

_____

_____

_____

_____

6. What can you do to help your students remember the vocabulary you teach them? _____

_____

_____

_____

_____

_____

_____

_____

_____

_____

Chapter 5: Comprehension

Discussion

Comprehension can be a complex process to identify and define. What does it mean to *you*? Comprehension has to do with *meaning*—deriving meaning from what we hear and what we read. Our ability to comprehend text depends on our understanding of the vocabulary, our previous experience and knowledge of the content, the simplicity or complexity of the text structure, our ability to hold onto the presented information and connect it with previous learning, and our language skills. This sounds complicated and it is! Teaching comprehension is not easy!

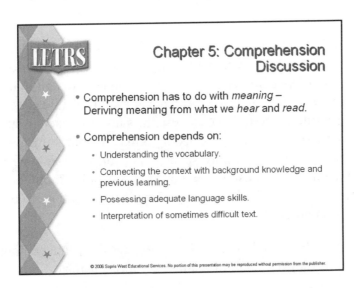

For many years, educators thought that comprehension happened as a natural outcome of the ability to read. We have since learned that this is not the case. Specific strategy instruction is required to teach the reader how to gain information from the text he reads, how to expand learning beyond the text, and how to combine meaning from several sources. More than likely, this intensive strategy instruction will take place within the classroom with whole-group instruction. *ParaReading* provides guidelines to help the paraeducator *support* the development of reading comprehension skills. Simple prompting or questioning before reading, during reading, and after reading can help students understand text as they read. Additionally, asking students to tell about what they have just read sends a message to students that what they are reading is important. Attending to the content and recalling the content of what they read plays an important role in comprehension.

Your Turn to Learn

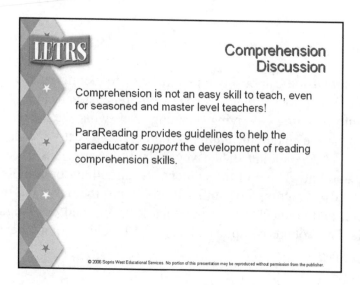

LETRS

Comprehension
Discussion

Comprehension is not an easy skill to teach, even for seasoned and master level teachers!

ParaReading provides guidelines to help the paraeducator *support* the development of reading comprehension skills.

© 2006 Sopris West Educational Services. No portion of this presentation may be reproduced without permission from the publisher.

You can help children improve comprehension skills when they read material or when you read to them. When children read, they exercise *reading comprehension*. When you read to children, they use *listening comprehension*. Whichever avenue a child uses to access the written material, we can use the same approach to support the development of comprehension skills. If your students have low reading skills, you may spend a portion of your time reading to them. You can use this opportunity to apply comprehension prompts. A prompt is a question or inquiry that initiates the comprehension process.

When the child reads material to you, use the same prompts to support the development of reading comprehension.

How is *your* comprehension? Let's do a little role-playing and try out a few comprehension prompts and strategies.

Tutors Know! *Reading Comprehension:* understanding what we read ourselves. Listening Comprehension: understanding what someone else reads to us!

Exercise #23: Background Experience

Your trainer will show you something to read. The experience will impress you with the important role that our personal experience brings to our ability to understand what we read.

1. What happened when you first read the selection? How did that change when you saw the title of the selection? What does this mean for our students and their ability to comprehend what they read?

   _____

   _____

   _____

   _____

2. Let's try it again with another selection. This time your trainer will prepare you for the reading, give you some background knowledge, and ask questions to help you understand the content. Record the comprehension *prompts* that are used before, during, and after the reading. A prompt is a question or inquiry that initiates the comprehension process.

   Before reading: _____

   _____

   During reading: _____

   _____

   After reading: _____

   _____

3. Tell about your experience with comprehension *this* time. How was it different from the first reading? Which reading example were you most comfortable with as a learner?

   _____

   _____

   _____

4. What other clues do authors provide for us that can be used to prepare young readers for what they will be reading?

   _____

   _____

How to Teach It: Comprehension

Predict, Apply, Retell

You will learn how to use three strategies to help your students improve their reading comprehension:

- ♦ Predict

- ♦ Apply background knowledge (previous experience)

- ♦ Retell

These strategies are typically used before reading, during reading, and after reading. Each one has prompts or questions associated with it.

Predict:

- ♦ "Tell me what you think will happen in this story."

- ♦ "What do you think will happen next?"

Apply Background Knowledge:

- ♦ "Tell me what you know about *(fill in the blank with something from the reading selection)*."

- ♦ "Has this every happened to you?"

Retell:

- ♦ "Tell me all about what you just read."

- ♦ "Tell me two things that you learned from your reading."

Key Point: As a tutor, your role will be to hold students accountable for reading for meaning. The simple questions and prompts that you use will send the message that when we read, we read to learn something! It is important to read for meaning and to remember!

> **Tutors Know!** Tutors ask simple questions and talk about text meaning to help children understand that we read to learn!

Exercise #24

Do this activity with a partner. Consider the strategies above to answer these questions.

1. Which questions or prompts could you use *before reading*?

   _____

   _____

   _____

   _____

2. Which questions or prompts could you use *while the student is reading*?

   _____

   _____

   _____

   _____

3. Which questions or prompts could you use *when the student has finished reading*?

   _____

   _____

   _____

   _____

Share and discuss your answers with the group.

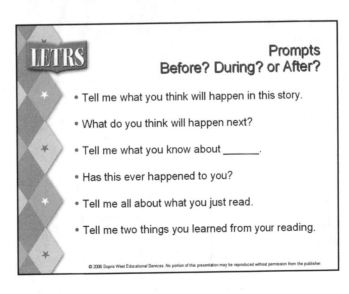

LETRS

**Prompts
Before? During? or After?**

• Tell me what you think will happen in this story.

• What do you think will happen next?

• Tell me what you know about _____.

• Has this ever happened to you?

• Tell me all about what you just read.

• Tell me two things you learned from your reading.

Practice It: Comprehension

You have learned three strategies that will form the basis for your focus on improving comprehension skills. Recall that comprehension is not an easy skill to teach because of the many language and processing skills that we use to gain meaning from text. The following activity will give you the opportunity to practice with your partner. You will work together to develop the prompts for each of the three strategies. Then, each of you will take a turn being the tutor or the student to try out the comprehension questions that you developed.

Read through each story together. Work together to develop your comprehension plan. Indicate whether your prompts will be used before, during, or after reading.

Story #1: Fooling Around

Rain and Wind sat resting on a mountain top. The sun was out, and there wasn't a cloud in the sky. Wind and Rain could see the people in the small town at the bottom of the mountain. Kids were playing in the park. People were sitting in the sun reading the Sunday paper. Everyone seemed happy.

Wind and Rain began to get bored because they didn't have anything to do. Wind said, "See me make the people run." Then Wind sent hats and papers flying down the street. Wind laughed, "What fun!"

Rain said, "I can make the people run too." So, Rain made black clouds. Soon big drops of water began falling. Rain laughed as the people ran for shelter.

(continued) **Story #1:** Fooling Around

Now develop two prompts for each strategy. For each prompt, indicate if you will use it before, during, or after reading the story.

Predict:

   1. _____

      _____

      _____

   2. _____

      _____

      _____

Apply Background Knowledge:

   1. _____

      _____

      _____

   2. _____

      _____

      _____

Retell:

   1. _____

      _____

      _____

   2. _____

      _____

      _____

Story #2: A Chicken's Life

Every chicken begins life the same way—as an egg. This is what happens. A hen and rooster mate. The hen lays between seven and fifteen eggs. Then the hen sits on the eggs until they hatch.

Once the hen lays the eggs, little chicks begin to form inside each of the eggs. At the start, the chicks seem to be little red specks on the eggs. In time, the specks get bigger.

After two days, you can see the heads of the chicks forming. After seven days, you can see the beginnings of their legs and wings. The chicks keep developing. Soon you can see their beaks. All this time, the mother hen sits on her nest.

After twenty-one days in the eggs, the little chicks run out of food. They become so big that they need to get out of their shells. "Peck, peck, peck."

All chicks have a tooth, called an egg tooth. The egg tooth helps them crack their shells. When they get out, the chicks are dripping wet and not very pretty. After a short time they fluff up. Soon they can eat and get around by themselves. "Cheep, cheep, cheep." Before long, the little chicks become roosters and hens.

Tutors Know! Prompt: a prepared question or query that is used to lead discussion of a reading selection.

Now develop two prompts for each strategy. Indicate for each prompt if you will use it before, during, or after reading the story.

Predict:

1. _____

   _____

   _____

2. _____

   _____

   _____

Reprinted by permission of the publisher from Marilyn Sprick, Lisa Howard, and Ann Fidanque, *Read Well Level One* (Longmont, CO: Sopris West, 1999), Unit 37, Story 5, pp. 42–43, © 2004 by Marilyn Sprick, Lisa Howard, and Ann Fidanque.

(continued) **Story #2:** A Chicken's Life

Apply Background Knowledge:

1. _____

   _____

   _____

2. _____

   _____

   _____

Retell:

1. _____

   _____

   _____

2. _____

   _____

   _____

Share your prompts with the group. How do they compare? Do you hear other prompts that you would like to use? Write them here:

_____

_____

_____

_____

_____

_____

Use your prepared prompts to role-play student and tutor. When you are the tutor, record student successes and/or any concerns you may have with your student's responses.

Error Response

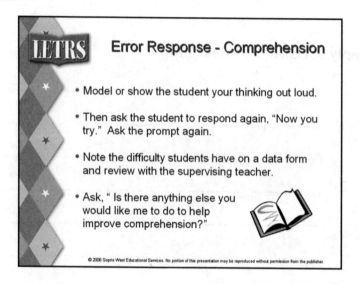

If your student is having difficulty with comprehension try the following:

◆ Model or show the student your thinking out loud as you answer the question or prompt. Then, ask the student to respond again: "Now you try." Ask the question again.

◆ On your data sheet, note the difficulty your student is having and share this information with your supervising teacher. Ask if there is anything else the teacher would like you to do during your tutor sessions to help improve comprehension.

Data Recording

Comprehension—*(circle one)* **Listening or Reading**

Student does this well: *(circle)*

predicts, applies background knowledge, retells

Student has difficulty with / I had to help the student with:

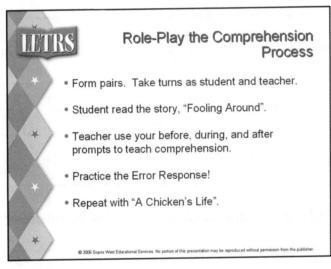

Discuss your teaching comprehension experiences with your group and trainer. Your trainer will help you prepare for the chapter assessment.

Review: Comprehension

1. What are three comprehension strategies that you can use to increase reading comprehension?

_____

_____

_____

2. At what times during a student's reading will you apply your comprehension instruction?

_____

_____

_____

_____

3. What is the difference between listening comprehension and reading comprehension?

_____

_____

_____

_____

_____

4. What is a prompt? Give three examples of prompts, one for each strategy covered in the lesson.

_____

_____

_____

_____

_____

_____

_____

_____

_____

_____

_____

_____

(continued) **Review:** Comprehension

5. How will you respond if your student has difficulty or makes an error? _____

_____

_____

_____

_____

_____

_____

_____

_____

_____

_____

_____

_____

_____

_____

_____

_____

Tutor's Tips

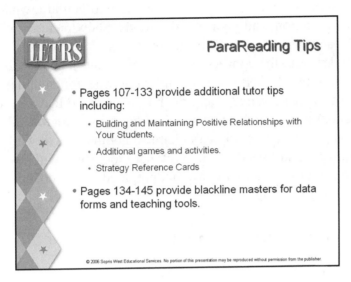

In this section you will find advice on how to *build positive relationships* with students, improve your *communication* with supervising teachers, and *organize* your student materials and time, as well as general tips to improve your instruction methods. You will also find ready-to-copy tutor *Strategy Reference Cards* for each of the five component areas you learned about. The data forms, phonics grids, etc., that you used during your training are also available in this section for you to copy.

Building and Maintaining Positive Relationships with Your Students

The relationships you establish with your students will contribute to the outcomes of your work with them. Building a sense of trust, safety, and security at the outset of your work with a child is critical to creating an environment where he or she feels comfortable taking risks. Chances are pretty good that the students with whom you will work have experienced reading failure in the past, which results in poor self-esteem and low confidence with reading tasks. They probably avoid reading because of repeated efforts to get better, without improvement. This can be a challenge for both the tutor and student at the start of a tutoring relationship. Here are some tips to help you get off to a positive start by building a safe and secure environment where students will be more open to taking risks and thus to becoming confident learners.

Set the Stage—Introduce Yourself

Start by introducing yourself. Talk about who you are, what you do for recreation, and your favorite foods. Show pictures of your family and pets. As you share these things about yourself, draw the student into the conversation: "Do you have a pet?" "Tell me about your family." "If you could have one wish for anything what would you wish? Why?" Help them to understand that you really care about what you do and about helping them learn to read. "We are going to have to work really hard sometimes. I will work hard to help you, and I need you to work hard too. But I will never ask you to do something that I have not prepared you to do, and I will be right here to help you."

Be Specific With Your Praise!

Sometimes, "Good job!" and "Excellent!" can lose their meaning. *Try to give specific praise that describes what the student did.* Here are some responses to a sampling of correct and incorrect student responses:

Phonemic Awareness Lesson

Student's Work	Tutor's Response
Student segments the sounds in a word correctly.	"Wow! You heard each of the sounds in that word and showed them to me."
Student gets stuck on segmenting the sounds in a word or does the task incorrectly.	"I heard you say the first and second sounds right." (Repeat them.) "Let me show you all of the sounds." (Do it for the student, and then have student do it alone.)
Student says he is bored with the lesson that you have prepared and are delivering.	"I know this seems boring to you, but let's get through it so that I can listen to you read!" Or: "Let's go through it quickly so we can move on." (Then pick up the pace.)
Student responses are all correct.	"I noticed that you were really paying attention during that part. You got them all right!"

Phonics Lesson

Student's Work	Tutor's Response
Student taps the letter sounds in her words and reads the words correctly.	"Great tapping those sounds! That helped you figure out the word."
Student guesses at the word and reads it incorrectly.	"The first sound was right on that word. Listen while I tap it." (Tap the word.) "Now you tap it with me. We'll come back to that one again later."
Student spells a word correctly.	"Way to match those sounds and letters! I can tell that you are getting better!"
Student spells a word incorrectly.	"The first part of the word is spelled right. Let me show you the right spelling." (Spell it, say the sounds and letters out loud, and underline or highlight the corrected parts. Have the student compare and trace your work, saying it as he spells it.) "When we say it as we spell it, it helps us remember. I bet you'll remember it next time!"

Fluency Lesson

Student's Work	Tutor's Response
Student improves his time on the second reading.	"I noticed that you were really concentrating during that reading. Look how far you read!"
Student does poorly on the first reading or worse on the second reading.	"Wow, that seemed hard for you. Let's read it together." (Read it aloud with the student, having the student follow with a marker or his finger.) "Now, try it again!" (If student still struggles, the passage may be too hard. Find an easier reading level.)

Vocabulary Lesson

Student's Work	Tutor's Response
Student uses a Wonder Word incorrectly.	"I can see how you would think that is a correct use for that word. Let me use it in a sentence for you." Or: "Tell me more to show you know the meaning."
Student uses a Wonder Word correctly.	"That is a great way to use the word _____!"
Student illustrates the word.	"Great way to show you know the meaning of _____. Tell me about your picture and use the word again."

Comprehension Lesson

Student's Work	Tutor's Response
Student provides an appropriate response to an inquiry.	"You were really thinking while you were reading! Great way to tell about what you read."
Student does not respond correctly or does not know the answer to your question.	"I can see that you are trying to remember what you read. Let's read this part again and see if we can come up with a good answer."
At the end of the tutoring session:	"Thank you for your hard work today. I can tell that you are improving by how many words you read right today." Or: "I can tell that you are improving by how often I got to see your bright cheery smile!"

Organization

Keeping yourself organized can be a challenge! Here are some tips to help you:

◆ Create a three-ring notebook for each of your students in which to organize materials. Have the students create a colorful cover for their notebook.

◆ Create sections in the notebook for each of the five components and for data forms. Use these sections to compile your teaching tools and collect examples of the student's work.

◆ Review the lesson and prepare materials before you work with the student. This sounds pretty elementary, but to do it takes time and planning!

◆ Keep a notepad in each student notebook for the purpose of recording questions, student observations, and general comments that you will use as a guide for communicating with your supervising teacher.

Communication

Sometimes it is hard for tutors to know when to initiate communication with supervisors, to recognize and then communicate what is needed, or even what to say to them! Keep these tips in mind right from the start:

◆ Identify the individual who will be the main contact person for questions and guidance.

◆ Do not hesitate to ask questions!

◆ Arrange a regular weekly meeting time with the contact person and decide with him/her what the purpose of your meetings will be. This meeting content could include a review of student data, setting goals, a preview of upcoming lessons, the opportunity to express explicit and general impressions of how the sessions are progressing, and a discussion of responses to behavioral issues.

◆ Confidentiality—Keep in mind at all times that the students with whom you work are protected under privacy and confidentiality codes. Do not discuss your students with anyone except your main contact person or other teachers who work with the students. Limit these discussions to the content of their reading lessons, their progress, and how to improve your instruction. Protect the students' notebooks and other data-collection materials. Respect families and individuals as you would want others to respect you and your family members.

Additional Tips

Instructional and interpersonal tips gleaned from the experience of veteran paraeducators and teachers are included in this section. Instructional tips are arranged by reading component to allow easy reference as the need arises for a new and different way to practice a skill! You may want to add some of these to your Strategy Reference Cards (available later in the workbook).

General

♦ Keep a variety of items available that you can use as manipulatives for phoneme lessons. Fish and teddy-bear crackers, one-inch blocks, colored paper squares, colored discs from math kits, dry beans, and flat beads are a few of the items you could keep in reclosable bags.

♦ Always have a couple of books at hand to read to the student. There may be times when the child doesn't feel well, or she may earn a special moment with you, or you may have extra time. Use these times to read to the child. Take advantage of the situation and apply some of your vocabulary and comprehension activities to improve listening comprehension.

♦ Provide an agenda for students. List the planned lesson components and the amount of time you intend to devote to each on a white board or sheet of paper. Let the student check off the components as you finish them. This can be extremely helpful with students who like to know what's expected of them.

Phonemic Awareness

Remember that with any phoneme activity, students acquire awareness of the phonemes in words in a predictable sequence. They begin by isolating the first sounds, then the last sounds, and then they develop the more difficult ability to isolate middle sounds in words. At the same time students are developing this awareness, they are learning to do *complete segmentation* with words (/m//a/ /n/) and *blending* (hearing /m//a//n/ and saying *man*).

Games

Develop game boards to practice phonemic awareness. Bingo, concentration, and tic-tac-toe are three good games to start with. Use pictures instead of words on the game boards. Students match pictures that have the same initial, ending, or middle sounds, whichever you instruct them to listen for. Ask your supervising teacher for a good source of pictures to choose from.

Eat Your Words!

1. Say a word containing two to four sounds. Have students move small crackers into a line, one for each sound, saying the sounds as they separate out all of the sounds in the word.

2. Instruct the student to "Eat the /s/" or "Eat the /m/."

3. Push away the crackers and do another word.

Simple Warm-ups

♦ **Robot Talk**—This is an exercise for auditory blending. Say a word *segmented* with every phoneme separated by about a second of time. The students then repeat the word back to you, blending the sounds as a whole unit. Use words from your lesson: "/s/ /t/ /r/ /ee/ /t/… *street*!"

♦ **Thumbs up! Thumbs Down!**—Students are asked to put their thumbs up when they hear a given sound in the word that the teacher says. Thumbs go down if the sound is not present.

"Listen for the sound /ōō/, like in *moon*." Say several words, some with /ōō/, such as *spoon*, *loon*, *boom*, *coop*, and others without the /ōō/ sound. Students put their thumbs up when they hear words with the /ōō/ sound. Say the word and the sound together as a group after the thumbs go up. "Spoon, /ōō/."

♦ **Riddles**—Play this word activity with a focus on different phoneme positions.

"I'm thinking of something good to eat. It *starts* with /p/." (pizza, pickles, pineapple)

"I'm thinking of something in the room that *ends* with /r/. It is in your desk." (eraser, marker, sticker)

"I'm thinking of someone's name that has the /ŏ/ sound *in* it." (Tom)

♦ **Make a Collection**—Begin this activity by telling the students that they are going to collect certain things today. The only things they can collect are things that start with a sound, end with a sound, or have a middle sound that you provide. (Use just one of the criteria.)

"Let's start our collection with things that have a middle (vowel) sound /ă/." (cat, mat, fan, rat, can, etc.)

Phonics

Practice and Review with Simple Games

Play games that require a lot of reading of words from the students' lessons. Ideas for these games include:

♦ **Bingo**—Write words on flash cards and also randomly on a sheet of paper that has been divided into a 4 x 4 grid. You and the student take turns picking a card and reading it. A marker is placed on the word. First one to get a row filled reads the words back to you.

♦ **Concentration**—Make a set of flash cards with each word written on two cards. Deal the cards face down on the table. Take turns turning over a card, reading it, and then turning over a second card and reading it. If they match, the reader takes the cards. With young students, limit the number of words to around five (ten cards total) and use two different colors for the cards, say, green and blue. (Therefore, a green card would have a match with a blue card.)

♦ **Go Fish**—Use flash cards as playing cards. Write the words across the top so that when the child is holding the cards, the words are visible across the top. Or use a folder as a privacy screen, and allow students to lay out their cards on the table. "Do you have *cute*?" "Go fish!"

Construct Collections of Words from the Reading Program

These can be done on a poster or on colored paper that is placed in the student's notebook. Group words that share the same phonic element—for example, words that have the ow spelling. Review these regularly. Draw attention to the sound that the words share and then to the spelling.

Make a Word Book

Provide a simple book of stapled folded sheets of paper, and help students create their own word book. Students write the grapheme that you are introducing at the top of the page. After the lesson, students write words from the lesson that have the identified grapheme. Have them choose a word to illustrate to help them remember the sound that the grapheme makes. Students could also write sentences using the words.

Multisensory Experiences

Provide opportunities for students to see, hear, and touch letters in words. These activities can get students moving around and can vary the lesson to maintain attention.

♦ **Tracing**—This is a common multisensory practice. Students have a word written in front of them. Tracing with a pencil or crayon, students *see* each letter as they *say* the sound, as they *trace* the shape of the letter. Immediately after saying all of the sounds, they should blend the whole word.

♦ **Large Arm Movements**—Present a word visually, read it, then spell it in the air with large arm movements that start from the shoulder. Say each letter as it is created in the air. Then read the whole word.

♦ **Salt Tray**—Line a paper box lid with colored paper. Apply a thin layer of salt. Students draw letters as they say the letter names or sounds in the salt. Gently shake the lid to erase.

♦ **Waxed Pipe Cleaners**—Students can bend waxed pipe cleaners (available at craft and school supply stores) into letter shapes. These letter shapes will stick on slick surfaces such as desktops, windows, and notebook covers. Have students arrange the pipe-cleaner letters into words as you dictate them. Instruct students to use their finger to trace the letters in the words as the sounds or letter names are said aloud. Blend the whole word when done.

Flash Cards

The use of flash cards will probably be a mainstay of your teaching methods. There are several ways to get the most from flash cards. Remember these suggestions and practice them so that they become habit!

♦ Write words from your reading lessons on the flash cards. The words should represent sets that share the same phonic element—for example, all words with the silent-e pattern.

♦ Maintain a quick and lively pace! Hold the set in one hand with the front facing the student while your other hand moves the cards to the back of the deck or to another separate pile on the table. If your student does not automatically read the word, help him decode it and read it, and then move it to the back of the deck. "You'll see this word again in a minute!" You can also "hide" it somewhere in the middle of the pile. Student gets to keep all words that are read quickly and accurately in his own pile on the table. This makes a game out of a very effective practice tool.

♦ Hold the cards so that all students in a group see the words. Instruct students to read the words chorally, at the same time, by giving them a cue: "What word?" Vary this by occasionally calling on an individual. "Get ready... Joe. Get ready... Mary. Get ready... Everybody!" Keep the pace moving.

♦ Store flash cards in envelopes labeled with the phonic element represented by the words. Let students take them home to practice or to keep when they know them well.

Fluency

Repeated readings will be your most common method of fluency training. Here are a few other ideas to increase reading opportunities for your students.

♦ **Choral Reading**—Group reads together aloud.

♦ **Echo Reading**—Group reads aloud phrase-by-phrase or sentence-by-sentence, repeating after a live or taped model. Follow along in the text with a marker or with your finger.

♦ **Shared Reading**—Tutor reads aloud *with* the child, maintaining a steady fluent pace for the child to keep up with.

◆ **Partner Reading**—Student *takes turns* reading aloud with the tutor, who provides help with word identification and feedback. Each reader follows along as the other reads.

◆ **Auditory Modeling**—Students are given exposure to modeling of fluent reading. By listening to fluent reading, students learn how a reader's voice attends to punctuation, mood, and pacing.

Vocabulary

Play games with the Wonder Words that students collect.

◆ **I'm Thinking**—Choose several words from the students' collections. Ask riddle questions for students to answer.

"I'm thinking of a word that I would use when I am really happy."

"I'm thinking of a word that means the opposite of big."

◆ **Concentration**—Match words with their meanings. Create matching cards with the word on one card and the meaning, or a sentence using that word, on another card. Deal words together face down on one side of the work space and meanings face down on the other side of the work space. Students take turns trying to match words with meanings.

◆ **Game Board Vocabulary**—Write the Wonder Words on cards and place them in a box or bag. Have a student draw a card from the box or bag; if she can use the word on the card correctly in a sentence that shows she understands the meaning, she then rolls dice and moves on a game board.

Comprehension

◆ **Draw a Picture**—Discuss favorite parts of the reading. Provide students with paper and crayons and let them illustrate their favorite parts. Make sure that you have ample time for this activity. Instruct students to retell the favorite parts when they are through with their drawings.

◆ **Order the Story**—Rewrite the main parts of the story in brief sentences, one per strip of paper. Mix up the strips and instruct students to place the strips in order to retell the story.

♦ **Buddy Tell**—After reading, pair students. Instruct one student to tell the other student everything they remember about the story. When the student is finished, have the listening student to share any information that might have been left out.

Strategy Reference Cards

The teaching tools that you learned during your training are organized here in separate reproducible boxes. Laminate or print on stiff paper and place on a ring for handy reference as you teach. You may wish to add some of the previous Tutor's Tips to your collection!

Strategy Reference Card #1

Phonemic Awareness

Choose 10 single-syllable words from the student text.

♦ **Isolate Initial Sounds**—Say the word and ask student to say the word and the first sound in that word. Repeat the word and sound with the student.

♦ **Isolate Final Sounds**—Say the word and ask the student to say the word and the last sound in that word. Repeat the word and the sound with the student.

♦ **Isolate Middle Sounds**—Say the word and ask the student to say the word and the middle sound in that word. Repeat the word and the sound with the student. Make sure that the words you choose for this have a distinguishable middle sound; three-sound words work best. If a student has difficulty here, use markers to segment the word and have student identify and say the middle sound using the markers.

♦ **Complete Segmentation**—Say a word and ask student to tell you all of the little sounds in that word.

♦ **"Secret" Language (Auditory Blending)**—Say a word segmented into its isolated sounds, and ask the student to say the "secret word" back to you.

Phonemic Awareness–Segmentation

Multisensory Cues:

♦ *Tap the Sounds*—Beginning with your index finger, tap once for each sound as you move through each finger.

♦ *Tap Head, Waist, Ankles*—To help students isolate middle sounds, use three-sound words and tap your head for the first sound, your waist for the middle sound, and then reach down to your feet for the last sound.

♦ *Finger Count*—Count and say the sounds one at a time, raising a finger for each one.

♦ *Pull the Sounds Out of Your Mouth*—Starting at your lips, pretend to grasp each isolated sound as you move your thumb and forefinger in a pulling movement away from your mouth.

♦ *Use Manipulatives*—Use little crackers, paper squares, or game pieces to help children see the segmentation as they separate the sounds in words.

Strategy Reference Card #3

Phonemic Awareness Data Recording

When you are teaching phonemic awareness, pay close attention to your students' responses. When errors are made, note what kinds of errors they are making:

♦ Are they able to do complete phoneme segmentation?

♦ Are they able to auditorially blend the phoneme-separated words that you give them?

♦ Are they confusing sounds? Example: saying /b/ for /p/, or /t/ for /d/.

♦ Do they consistently miss the last sounds or middle sounds in words?

Phonics–Whole-Word Blending

Another name for this procedure is "touch and say." Children touch each letter (or grapheme), say the sounds and then blend the sounds to read the word.

Step-by-step procedure for decoding shack:

1. Point to the digraph *sh* and say, "Sound"; students say "/sh/."

2. Point to the *a* and say, "Sound"; students say "/a/."

3. Point to the *ck* and say, "Sound"; students say "/k/."

4. Slide finger under the whole word to blend it; students say, "*Shack*".

5. Point to the word and say, "The word is *shack*."

6. Check for understanding of the word and the ability to use it in a sentence.

Phonics–Stretch-and-Say Blending

Phonemes are segmented and counted and then the whole word is blended with an accompanying gesture to pull the sounds together into the word.

Step-by-step procedure for decoding *sun*:

1. Say the whole word, "Sun."

2. Ask students to hold up one finger for each sound they hear as the word is segmented and the phonemes counted.

3. Say the whole word while pulling arm down or sweeping it across your body from left to right.

Phonics–Tap and Blend

This method is similar to Whole-Word Blending except that the student is actively involved with the decoding process through tapping the sounds as tutor and student work through the word together.

Step-by-step procedure for decoding *stick*:

In unison, tutor and student tap index finger and thumb together as they say each sound in the word and blend the sounds together. If needed, the tutor can touch each grapheme as the student taps the sounds.

1. Tap and say "/s/."

2. Tap and say "/t/."

3. Tap and say "/ĭ/."

4. Tap and say "/k/."

5. Run finger under whole word and say, "Stick."

Strategy Reference Card #7

Phonics–Sounds to Spelling

The student separates the sounds in a word and then applies the grapheme for those sounds. That is, the student spells the word.

You will need the following materials:

♦ Copies of the Sounds to Spelling form or a sheet of paper with boxes and lines.

♦ Moveable sound markers—paper squares or little crackers, some small items that the students can use to represent the separate phonemes.

♦ Words from the student's reading materials.

Step-by-step procedure for decoding *book*:

1. Tutor says, "Book."

2. Student repeats the word and moves markers into the spaces for each separate sound, saying the sounds as the markers are touched and moved—" /b/ /ŏŏ/ /k/."

3. The tutor asks two types of questions about the sounds: "Show me the /k/," and then, pointing to the second sound marker, "What is this sound?" Student says, "/ŏŏ/."

   These two questions can be repeated for different sounds in the word so that the student is responding to questions about all of the represented sounds.

4. Once the questions have been asked, the student is instructed to push up the markers one at a time and write the graphemes for each sound in the spaces, saying the sounds as the letters are written.

5. The student then writes the entire word on the line.

Phonics—Individual Letter Sounds

Materials: Moveable letters (letters written on flash cards or actual letter shapes).

1. "This letter *m* makes the sound /m/. Say it with me, /m/. What sound does the *m* (pointing) make?" "When we see *m* in a word, we say /m/."

Follow the same process for each letter, teaching the sounds.

2. Point randomly to the letters, asking for the sounds. Point and say, "What sound?" Keep a quick pace. Make it lively: "I am going to try to trick you…."

3. Ask the student to show you a given sound. "Show me the /s/. Show me the /ă/."

In the group of letters you are teaching, use 70% letter sounds the child knows and 30% letter sounds the child is learning.

Fluency–Repeated Readings

Materials: Stopwatch, a repeated readings chart, three different colored pencils or markers, a reading passage that is written at the child's instructional level, and a copy of the reading passage on which to mark errors.

Step-by-Step Process: Instruct the student: "Please read this passage for your fluency training today. Begin reading here (point), and read until I tell you to stop. If you come to a word you don't know, I will tell you the word." Time him for one minute, and note the number of words he reads. Subtract the errors for a total of words read correctly per minute (WCPM).

1. Chart the WCPM on the repeated readings chart. Show the student how to graph his own performance.

2. Review the errors with the student. Show and tell him the words you helped him with, words he omitted or substituted, and words he hesitated with.

3. Instruct the student to read the passage again, and follow the same procedure.

4. Do this for a total of three times marking the errors with a different color each time. Have student graph his performance after each reading. Work with the student to set goals between readings—"How many words can you read next time? Can you beat your time?"

Fluency–Repeated Readings:
How do you know what text to use?

♦ If your students are just beginning to learn **letter sounds**, repeated readings are to be done with a page of letters from which letter sounds will be read.

♦ If your students are **decoding and blending single words** to practice building automaticity, do repeated readings with isolated words that reflect the target decoding skills you are working on.

♦ Once your students are reading **passages of text, such as paragraphs and stories**, use these texts for repeated readings. This level of repeated reading generally begins around mid-first grade.

Strategy Reference Card #11

Fluency—What To Count As Errors When Doing Repeated Readings

Errors:

♦ *Unknown word.* The student hesitates or attempts to read a word but does not produce the correct word in three seconds. Provide the correct word for the student and mark it as an error on your sheet.

♦ *Substitution.* The student misreads a word, substituting a different word for the actual word in the text.

♦ *Omission.* The student leaves a word out while reading.

Not Errors:

♦ Rereading words or phrases.

♦ Self-corrections made within three seconds.

♦ Skipping a line. (Do not count the words in the omitted line as errors.)

Vocabulary

Vocabulary instruction begins with finding **Wonder Words** in reading material that you will be reading to the students or material that they will be reading themselves. Follow these steps:

- ◆ Preread the material that your students will be reading or that you will read to your students.

- ◆ Choose two words that meet the Wonder Words criteria: a) words or phrases that may be difficult to understand and that the students may hear or read again and therefore need to know; or b) words that may have multiple meanings.

- ◆ Show the written Wonder Words to the students. Read the words. "These are Wonder Words that you will be reading today."

- ◆ Read each word and provide definitions.

- ◆ Tell about the word using the context of the story.

- ◆ Have the students record a picture or brief definition in their Wonder Words journal to help recall the meaning.

- ◆ Instruct the students to read the passage.

Strategy Reference Card #13

Vocabulary

Tip—Revisit students' **Wonder Words** journals and discuss the words in relation to a story. Always encourage students to use the Wonder Words in their discussion. "Tell me about it, and use the word _____." Rephrase for the students if they do not use the Wonder Words. Provide opportunities for the students to apply the vocabulary to their own experiences.

Strategy Reference Card #14

Comprehension

These strategies are typically used before reading, during reading, and after reading. Each one has its own prompt or question associated with it.

Predict:

♦ "Tell me what you think will happen later in this story."

♦ "What do you think will happen next?"

Apply Background Knowledge:

♦ "Tell me what you know about (*fill in the blank with something from the reading selection*)."

♦ "Has this ever happened to you?"

Retell:

♦ "Tell me all about what you just read."

♦ "Tell me two things that you learned from your reading."

Strategy Reference Card #15

Vocabulary and Comprehension Error Response

If your student is having difficulty with vocabulary or comprehension try the following:

♦ Model or show the student *your* thinking out loud as you answer the question or prompt. Then, ask the student to respond again: "Now you try." Ask the question again.

♦ On your data sheet, note the difficulty your student is having and share this information with your supervising teacher. Ask if there is anything else the teacher would like you to do during your tutor sessions to help improve vocabulary or comprehension.

Strategy Reference Card #16

General Error Response

1. Point out one thing that was done correctly.

2. Demonstrate the correct way.

3. Point out the place where a correction was made. Explain.

4. Have the student do it again, with you.

Note the error on your data form.

Forms

Forms and blackline masters for many of the teaching tools used in the *ParaReading* training are included in this section.

- ♦ **Data Forms**—Three different forms are included. Choose one of these forms to use if there is not a data form included with your reading program. Record what your students do well and any concerns that arise during your tutoring sessions.

- ♦ **Sounds to Spelling Form**—This is a phonics lesson form that makes it easy to segment words by applying graphemes to the sounds in a word.

- ♦ **Fluency Training: Repeated Readings Chart**—Here is a form that can be used for three sessions of repeated readings. Each session records three readings of the same material.

- ♦ **Wonder Words Journal**—Copy several of these two-sided, then fold and staple and add a colorful cover to create a Wonder Words journal.

- ♦ **Phonics Grids**—Students use the empty grid to write graphemes in as you dictate them, and then cut them out to build words. The completed grids can be used to review and to cut and build words. Note that you may have to add extras of some letters if words contain many of the same letters.

- ♦ **LETRS Consonant and Vowel Articulation Charts**—Use these charts to practice saying phonemes in the phonemic awareness chapter.

Data Form 1

Student Name: _____

Monday **Date:** **Comments:**	**Sounds**—*Student does well: (circle)* initial, ending, middle, segmentation, blending *Student errors: (circle)* initial, ending, middle, segmentation, blending **Decoding**—*Student errors: (circle)* specific letter-sound correspondences, whole-word blending, letter-sound confusion **Fluency**—*Record WCPM:* 1st reading _____ 2nd reading _____ 3rd Reading _____ **Vocabulary**—Can the student use the vocabulary words in a sentence that shows he/she knows the word? Yes No **Comprehension**—*Student does well:(circle)* predicts, applies background knowledge, retells
Tuesday **Date:** **Comments:**	**Sounds**—*Student does well: (circle)* initial, ending, middle, segmentation, blending *Student errors: (circle)* initial, ending, middle, segmentation, blending **Decoding**—*Student errors: (circle)* specific letter-sound correspondences, whole-word blending, letter-sound confusion **Fluency**—*Record WCPM:* 1st reading _____ 2nd reading _____ 3rd Reading _____ **Vocabulary**—Can the student use the vocabulary words in a sentence that shows he/she knows the word? Yes No **Comprehension**—*Student does well:(circle)* predicts, applies background knowledge, retells
Wednesday **Date:** **Comments:**	**Sounds**—*Student does well: (circle)* initial, ending, middle, segmentation, blending *Student errors: (circle)* initial, ending, middle, segmentation, blending **Decoding**—*Student errors: (circle)* specific letter-sound correspondences, whole-word blending, letter-sound confusion **Fluency**—*Record WCPM:* 1st reading _____ 2nd reading _____ 3rd Reading _____ **Vocabulary**—Can the student use the vocabulary words in a sentence that shows he/she knows the word? Yes No **Comprehension**—*Student does well:(circle)* predicts, applies background knowledge, retells
Thursday **Date:** **Comments:**	**Sounds**—*Student does well: (circle)* initial, ending, middle, segmentation, blending *Student errors: (circle)* initial, ending, middle, segmentation, blending **Decoding**—*Student errors: (circle)* specific letter-sound correspondences, whole-word blending, letter-sound confusion **Fluency**—*Record WCPM:* 1st reading _____ 2nd reading _____ 3rd Reading _____ **Vocabulary**—Can the student use the vocabulary words in a sentence that shows he/she knows the word? Yes No **Comprehension**—*Student does well:(circle)* predicts, applies background knowledge, retells
Friday **Date:** **Comments:**	**Sounds**—*Student does well: (circle)* initial, ending, middle, segmentation, blending *Student errors: (circle)* initial, ending, middle, segmentation, blending **Decoding**—*Student errors: (circle)* specific letter-sound correspondences, whole-word blending, letter-sound confusion **Fluency**—*Record WCPM:* 1st reading _____ 2nd reading _____ 3rd Reading _____ **Vocabulary**—Can the student use the vocabulary words in a sentence that shows he/she knows the word? Yes No **Comprehension**—*Student does well:(circle)* predicts, applies background knowledge, retells

⭐ Data Form 2

Record student performance, data, and notes to communicate with student's teacher.

Student Name: _____

Week of:	Week of:	Week of:
Phonemic Awareness:	Phonemic Awareness:	Phonemic Awareness:
Phonics:	Phonics:	Phonics:
Fluency:	Fluency:	Fluency:
Vocabulary and Comprehension:	Vocabulary and Comprehension:	Vocabulary and Comprehension:

Data Form 3

Record student performance, data, and notes to communicate with student's teacher.

Student Name: _____

	MONDAY	TUESDAY	WEDNESDAY	THURSDAY	FRIDAY
Phonemic Awareness					
Decoding/Phonics					
Fluency					
Comprehension Vocabulary					

Student Name: _____

Sounds to Spelling

Fluency Training: Repeated Readings Chart

Student Name: _____

	Date: _____ Reading Selection: _____ _____			Date: _____ Reading Selection: _____ _____			Date: _____ Reading Selection: _____ _____		
Words Read Correctly Per Minute									
120									
100									
90									
80									
70									
60									
50									
40									
30									
20									
10									
0	1	2	3	1	2	3	1	2	3

Wonder Words

Wonder Words

Grid One

Grid One Completed

a apple	e echo	i itch	o octopus	u up		
a-e babe	i-e hive	o-e rose	u-e tube	u-e mule	e-e theme	
m man	p pump	s sun	b boy	t tame	d dog	f fun
l lap	r rabbit	n nose	w wish	h hair	c cat	k kite
j jam	g goat	g gym	c city	y yummy	v valentine	z zipper
qu quilt	x bo<u>x</u>					
ir shi<u>r</u>t	er sist<u>er</u>	ur <u>bur</u>p	ar arm	or corn		
au autumn	aw awesome	ai sail	ay day	ee bee	oa boat	oi oil
oy joy	ea See LETRS Vowel Chart	ou See LETRS Vowel Chart	ow See LETRS Vowel Chart	oo boot	oo book	ew chew
th <u>th</u>in	<u>th</u> <u>th</u>em	sh shoe	ch chin	ng ring		

Grid Two

o	u	i	a			
n	b	g	l	s	m	p
th	ng	sh				
aw	oo	ur	ee			
f	t					
r	c					

LETRS Vowel Chart

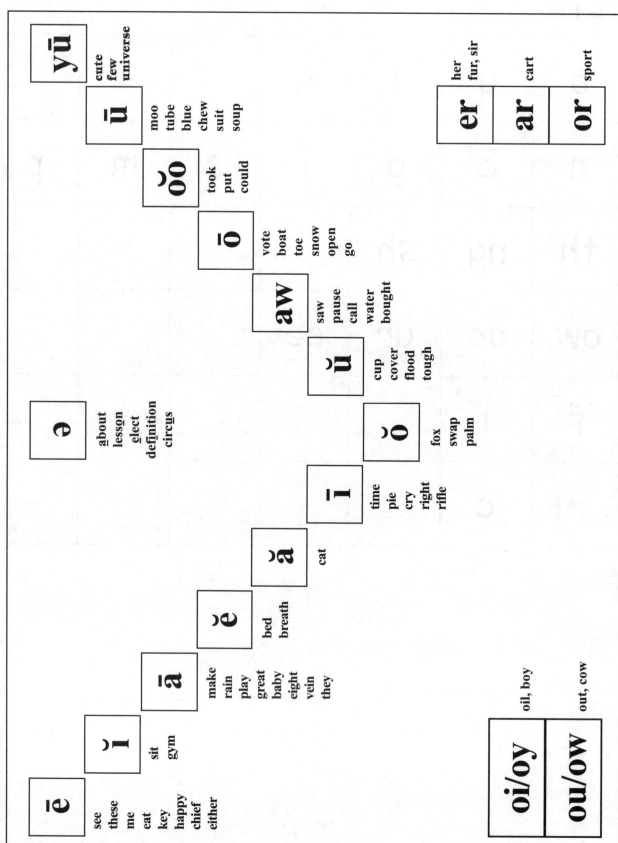

ē	see, these, me, eat, key, happy, chief, either
ĭ	sit, gym
ā	make, rain, play, great, baby, eight, vein, they
ĕ	bed, breath
ǎ	cat
ī	time, pie, cry, right, rifle
ŏ	fox, swap, palm
e	about, lesson, elect, definition, circus
ŭ	cup, cover, flood, tough
aw	saw, pause, call, water, bought
ō	vote, boat, toe, snow, open, go
ǒǒ	took, put, could
ū	moo, tube, blue, chew, suit, soup
yū	cute, few, universe

er	her, fur, sir
ar	cart
or	sport

oi/oy	oil, boy
ou/ow	out, cow

Consonant Phonemes by Place and Manner of Articulation

	Lips	Teeth/ Lips	Tongue/ Teeth	Ridge/ Teeth	Roof Mouth	Back of Throat	Glottis
Stops Unvoiced / Voiced	/p/ /b/			/t/ /d/		/k/ /g/	
Nasals	/m/			/n/		/ng/	
Fricatives Unvoiced / Voiced		/f/ /v/	/th/ /th/	/s/ /z/	/sh/ /zh/		
Affricates Unvoiced / Voiced					/ch/ /j/		
Glides Unvoiced / Voiced					/y/	/wh/ /w/	/h/
Liquids				/l/ /r/			

Reprinted by permission of the publisher from Louisa Moats, LETRS *Module 2*
(Longmont, CO: Sopris West, 2004), p. 36, © 2005 by Sopris West. Permission is granted to photocopy this page.

References

Adams, G., & Brown, S. (2004). *Six-minute solution: A reading fluency program*. Longmont, CO: Sopris West Educational Services.

Adams, M. J. (1990). *Beginning to read: Thinking and learning about print*. Cambridge, MA: MIT Press.

Biemiller, A. (1999). Language and reading success. In J. Chall (Ed.), *From Reading Research to Practice: A Series for Teachers*. Cambridge, MA: Brookline Books.

Bryson, B. (1990). *The mother tongue: English and how it got that way*. New York: Harper Collins.

Cohen, P. A., Kulik, J. A., & Kulik, C. C. (1982). Educational outcomes of tutoring: A meta-analysis of findings. *American Educational Research Journal, 19*, 237–248.

Edformation (2002). *AIMSWeb Benchmark Assessments*. Available at: www.edformation.com.

Elbaum, B., Vaughn, S., Hughes, M. T., & Moody, S. W. (2000). How effective are one-on-one tutoring programs in reading for elementary students at risk for reading failure? A meta-analysis of the intervention research. *Journal of Educational Psychology, 92*(4), 605–619.

Fitzgerald, J. (2001). Can minimally trained college student volunteers help young at-risk children read better? *Reading Research Quarterly, 36*(1), 28–47.

Foorman, B. R., Francis, D. J., Fletcher, J. M., Schatschneider, C., & Mehta, P. (1998). The role of instruction in learning to read: Preventing reading failure in at-risk children. *Journal of Educational Psychology, 90*(1), 37–55.

Glaser, D. R. (2002). *High school tutors: Their impact on elementary students' reading fluency through implementing a research-based instruction model*. Doctoral Dissertation: Boise State University.

Grace, K. (2007). *Phonics and spelling through phoneme grapheme mapping*. Longmont, CO: Sopris West Educational Services.

Hasbrouk, J. E., Ihnot, C., & Rogers, G. (1999). Read naturally: A strategy to increase oral reading fluency. *Reading Research Instruction, 39*(1), 27–37.

Moats, L. C. (2003). *The speech sounds of English: A video tutorial with Louisa Moats*. Longmont, CO: Sopris West Educational Services.

Moats, L. C. (1999). *Teaching reading is rocket science: What expert teachers of reading should know and be able to do*. Washington, DC: American Federation of Teachers.

Moats, L. C. (1999–2004). *Language essentials for teachers of reading and spelling* (LETRS). Longmont, CO: Sopris West Educational Services.

Moats, L. C. (2005). *Language essentials for teachers of reading and spelling* (LETRS) *Module one.* Presenter's CD-ROM by Carol Tolman. Longmont, CO: Sopris West Educational Services.

Mueser, K. T., Yarnold, P. R., & Foy, D. W. (1991). Statistical analysis for single-case designs: Evaluating outcome of imaginal exposure treatment of chronic PTSD. *Behavior Modification, 15*(2), 134–155.

Nagy, W. E., & Anderson, R. C. (1984). How many words are there in printed school English? *Reading Research Quarterly, 19*(3), 304-330.

No child left behind act of 2001: Executive summary. Washington, DC: U.S. Department of Education

Report of the National Reading Panel: Teaching children to read. (2000). Washington, DC: National Institutes of Health.

Shaywitz, S. (2003). *Overcoming dyslexia: A new and complete science-based program for reading problems at any level*. New York: Alfred A. Knopf.

Shinn, M. R., Deno, S. L., & Fuchs, L. S. (2002). *Using curriculum-based measurements in a problem-solving model*. New York: Guilford.

Sprick, M., Howard, L. M., & Fidanque, A. (1999). *Read Well*. Longmont, CO: Sopris West Educational Services.

U.S. Department of Education, (1999). Unpublished tabulations from the follow-up survey of state implementation of federal elementary and secondary education programs. In *The Jossey-Bass Reader on School Reform*. San Francisco; Jossey-Bass.

Vadasy, P. F., Jenkins, J. R., & Pool, K. (2000). Effects of tutoring in phonological and early reading skills on students at risk for reading disabilities. *Journal of Learning Disabilities*, *33*(4), 579–590.

Vellutino, F. R., & Scanlon, D. M. (1987). Phonological coding, phonological awareness, and reading ability: Evidence from a longitudinal and experimental study. *Merrill-Palmer Quarterly*; *33*(3), 321–63.

Wasik, B. A. (1998). Volunteer tutoring programs in reading; A review. *Reading Research Quarterly*, *33*(3), 266–292.